ACHIEVING A TRIPLE WIN

Traditionally, organizations have left Human Capital needs to the Human Resources department. However, the talent management landscape has changed. Managers have begun to recognize that attracting and employing highly talented individuals makes an enormous impact on the company's bottom line.

The 'Human Capital Cycle' model presented in *Achieving a Triple Win: Human capital management of the employee lifecycle* presents a more systematic and comprehensive approach to human capital management, based on the author's insight and experience into the connection between an organization's strategy and its human capital needs and plans. Focusing on the six stages of the employee lifecycle, the book emphasizes the need for a more adaptive, specialized approach to HRM to achieve what the author calls the 'Triple Win'—substantial benefits for customers, employees and the business as a whole. The book includes:

- rich descriptions and examples
- details on how to plan and execute each stage
- questions and issues
- case studies.

This book is a useful resource for senior leaders, decision makers, HR professionals, and those responsible for talent management in the private and public sectors. Students of HRM and management would find this an enlightening supplementary reading.

Joyce A. Thompsen holds a Ph.D. in applied management and decision sciences. She spent ten years as a corporate HR executive. At AchieveGlobal she consults with clients to optimize talent, and to clarify and execute strategy to achieve results.

ACHIEVING A TRIPLE WIN

Human capital management of the employee lifecycle

Joyce A. Thompsen

Routledge
Taylor & Francis Group

LONDON AND NEW YORK

First published 2010
by Routledge
2 Park Square, Milton Park, Abingdon, Oxon OX14 4RN

Simultaneously published in the USA and Canada
by Routledge
270 Madison Avenue, New York, NY 10016

Routledge is an imprint of the Taylor & Francis Group, an Informa business

© 2010 Joyce A. Thompsen

Typeset in Aldus and Gill Sans by
Florence Production Ltd, Stoodleigh, Devon
Printed and bound in Great Britain by
The MPG Books Group

British Library Cataloguing in Publication Data
A catalogue record for this book is available from the British Library

Library of Congress Cataloguing in Publication Data
A catalog record for this book has been requested

ISBN: 978–0–415–54834–2 (hbk)
ISBN: 978–0–415–54835–9 (pbk)
ISBN: 978–0–203–87520–9 (ebk)

CONTENTS

FIGURES

ACKNOWLEDGMENTS

Many professional colleagues share in the enthusiasm for the pursuit of a Triple Win and strategic application of human capital management throughout the employee lifecycle. My husband and loving partner for life, John R. Wright, Jr., is also a steadfast source of encouragement, personal support, and intellectual stimulation.

1

INTRODUCTION

As a business or governmental leader in a position of senior management, you might be wondering why you are reading this book. Traditionally, most organizations leave all Human Capital needs to the Human Resources department. Functions such as recruitment and selection, employee orientation, career growth, and employee departure all fall under the responsibility of a group of specialists trained to make decisions on such matters. There is a reason for this conventional wisdom: leaving all matters of personnel and talent management to a specialized team frees up the time and energy of senior management to focus on more "important" business issues. If they don't have to commit time to Human Capital concerns, after all, they can drive strategies to improve revenue, cut expenses, increase market share, and above all, keep the customer happy.

But that's just it. Traditional approaches are becoming more and more obsolete. Conventional wisdom doesn't look so conventional any more. The talent management landscape has changed. If a business or governmental leader hopes to keep up, he/she must change along with it.

The reason you are reading this book is simple: Human Capital Management has *become* a significant business issue for most organizations. And if it hasn't yet become an issue for your organization, it will in the very near future.

What is the reason for this shift? For one thing, many business and governmental leaders have begun to see the direct correlation between highly talented people and organizational success. The more talented people an organization employs, the more likely they are to create a cost-effective, high-quality, and appealing product or service (and to do it efficiently). Having a larger base of highly talented people *is* leverage—any organization that can get things done more efficiently and effectively than anyone else in the market space enjoys a direct and explicit advantage over the competition.

Time and time again, we have seen it: senior management teams that pay attention to Human Capital concerns see their organizations simply explode with measurable business success. The more they invest in attracting, employing, and maintaining highly talented people, the better the product or service, the happier the customer, the healthier the bottom line.

As you will see in the pages to come, the timing of this gradual shift in thinking is perhaps poor. In the coming years, the market for talented people will become incredibly competitive. In addition, a large cross-section of talented workers (the Baby Boomers) will soon reach the traditional age of retirement. Many businesses and governmental agencies will find themselves with more openings than they had anticipated and fewer qualified people with which to fill those openings.

Each year, the matter becomes more and more urgent. The time to expend the energy and resources it takes to implement and hone Human Capital Management practices is now. With so much on the line, this is no longer a Human Resources issue. This is a business issue that requires the attention of all members of senior management.

As a core business issue, Human Capital Management is inextricably linked with five emerging and business-driving trends, according to a 2007 study:[1]

- Globalization and the need for an international workforce
- Organizational growth
- Evolving or transforming cultures
- Changes in market demands
- Retirements.

Each of these trends requires active, strategic consideration and planning by all members at the executive table. In each case, Human Capital Management is an essential ingredient in the strategic solution and its execution.

With this book, we present the Human Capital Cycle. As you will see, it is a unique approach to the problem of attracting and keeping highly talented people in that it is more adaptive than anything ever applied to the problem before. Traditional Human Capital Management practices suggest a linear approach to a non-linear problem. Not every talented employee follows the standard career path any more. Highly talented people aren't as attracted to traditional recruitment methods as they used to be. And the task of keeping these people happy and committed to their employer is becoming more and more specialized. Like any effective business strategy, the Human Capital Cycle takes a fair amount of planning in the early stages if it is going to be effective. It might seem difficult at first, but that is another thing that separates the Human Capital Cycle from the rest of the pack: it is designed for clarity and ease of use over the long term. Make no mistake, once implemented, it will keep your Human Resources running smoother and more efficiently than it ever has before. As a result, your organization will experience substantial benefits for its customers, its employees, and its own business health—or what we call the Triple Win.

In the chapters that follow, we present data, case studies, and a high-powered Human Capital model that will drive organizational success over the long term. In order to protect trade secrets, all anecdotes presented in this book are fictionalized to some degree. The central story—that of Diane Limon and Sky International—is also fictional. It is a proxy of many major organizations who have shared data or otherwise worked with AchieveGlobal.

As a person in a position of senior management, if you apply the lessons presented in this book with vigor, your organization will see tremendous improvement in customer satisfaction, employee morale and productivity, and above all, financial success. With the Human Capital Cycle in place, you will be well on your way to experiencing the tremendous benefits of the Triple Win.

2

BROADENING THE
HUMAN CAPITAL SPECTRUM

As CHIEF EXECUTIVE OFFICER (CEO) of Sky International, the United States' top architecture firm in terms of revenue, Diane Limon understands the importance of talented individuals. It recently occurred to her that the level of talent at her company wasn't simply an important Human Resources (HR) issue to address; rather, she now realizes that the level of talent *dictates* the value of her company's product, the perception of its customers, and the level of financial success that it enjoys.

In 1982, Sky International was a simple firm of ten architects. An executive board had been formed around Limon and Harold Stevenson, acting chief financial officer (CFO). Plans to expand the company were being set in motion.

By the mid-1990s, Sky and its brain trust had begun to re-envision the company outlook. The hiring of a talented young visionary named Norma Gaffney brought to light the niche market of upscale condominiums in trendy city neighborhoods and the surrounding suburbs. In this same year, Sky would go public, raising the stakes for its investors and placing a far heavier burden on its talent pool. Of course, the acclaim for Gaffney's designs, coupled with the condominium boom of the late 1990s and early 2000s, would lead to a surge in growth for the firm. Sky now found work in cities in each corner of the United States, well outside its initial boundaries of the greater Cincinnati area. Satellite offices were established and hundreds of employees were hired.

Sky managed to attract the interest of perhaps the most talented architect in the United States, Steven Lions. The bold, unorthodox designs promised by Lions would open avenues to the kinds of high-art projects that Limon had always dreamed to be a part of. With Lions on board, Sky could now turn to the high-money, high-recognition world of designing artistic city centers. Thanks to this move, Limon was able to pick up her first copy of the annual Fortune 500 in which she and her company were featured. Truly, business had never been better—and the future certainly looked bright.

Prospects were good. Sales were up. Talent was high. Customer satisfaction could not have been better. So how could it be that Sky International's financials were slipping?

HUMAN CAPITAL MANAGEMENT: A CRITICAL BUSINESS ISSUE

When many members of senior management sit down to strategize on how to improve company figures, far too many overlook one core business issue: Human Capital. In the coming years, the business world stands to face a crisis unlike any before seen. Today, coupled with economic stressors, many organizations are experiencing the effects of an aging and restless workforce. Many have come to realize that the number of available and highly talented individuals is dwindling. Still others now recognize the substantial impact that a lack of talent can have on the bottom line.

Things have changed. Market demands have shifted. Corporate cultures continue to evolve. More companies are beginning to globalize. As these companies grow and search for a more international workforce, the market for talent has narrowed and become more competitive. Gone are the days when senior management can simply sit back and expect the HR team to guide new and talented individuals along a linear path of career development.

Given these trends, it is easy to see that Human Capital Management has become a core business issue. Data show that an organization hoping to sustain economic viability over the long term (and deliver on targeted results) depends greatly upon focused planning and management in the following two disciplines:

1. Building, deploying, and retaining highly talented performers and leadership bench strength.
2. Ensuring that the right people with the right skills are in the right place at the right time.[1]

The proper maintenance of these two disciplines of talent management, more often than not, *directly* correlates with company success. A study conducted by McKinsey & Company found talent management to be the most significant success factor for most organizations.[2] The study concluded that Human Capital proved more important from a business standpoint than even strategy, research and development (R&D), or financial capital.

The research of Baruch Lev, professor of accounting at New York University, suggests that the intangible assets contribution made by Human Capital accounts for more than 50 percent of the market capitalization enjoyed by public companies in the United States. Accenture estimates that, since the year 1980, the value of intangible assets has increased from 20 percent to 70 percent against the value of S&P 500 organizations.[3]

Despite these facts, too many organizations continue to put their Human Capital trust in a broken or outdated system. High-powered businesses need new and high-powered Human Capital strategies. The right strategy will help any organization meet the demands of an ever evolving marketplace—and it will lead directly to the Triple Win: improved value for the customer, the organization, and its employees.

THE AGING OF A TALENT POOL

Diane Limon was troubled. The quarterly financial numbers she had just received were far lower than expected. There was absolutely nothing to suggest that her company should have experienced a loss in the first quarter. Given historical trends, Sky International should have enjoyed the start of another remarkably successful year. It couldn't simply be that the company had peaked; there was still so much market share to be garnered. And in the previous year, they had unveiled their two most high-profile projects to date. There had been plenty of media buzz, plenty of positive feedback, and the sales department had reported a wave of new prospective clients.

So how was it possible that Limon was looking at her first unfavorable financial report in nearly a decade? With all the usual business aspects trending upward, only one potential contributing factor remained: the people who worked at her ever-expanding company must not have been performing at the expected level.

As Limon took a step back, the gravity of the Human Capital issue was not lost on her. Literally everything that her company did—literally every shred of success that it had ever experienced—depended entirely on the talent of her employees.

This idea was particularly harrowing when Limon realized that a significant portion of Sky International's prospects for continued and future success rested on the shoulders of only two people: Norma Gaffney and Steven Lions, her key architects. So much depended on their continued happiness. In addition to their obvious value as the creators of the company's highest profile products, these two brilliant minds had assembled a substantial support staff of highly talented and capable researchers, sketch artists, and marketers—all of whom were integral to the company's ability to deliver a high-quality product on a deadline.

What if either Gaffney or Lions became disgruntled? What if they departed for another company (or worse, founded their own competing firms)? And if they left, what would happen to all of their talented support staff?

Limon now found herself worrying about thousands of employees. There was the management at each of the eight satellite offices that had been established over the years. There was the senior management team. Specifically, there was Harold Stevenson. Without his tremendous leadership and invaluable business contacts, none of the success would have been possible in the first place.

When Limon examined things from this perspective, she realized that her disappointing quarterly numbers could have been predicted. If she had paid more attention to Human Capital concerns, it all might have been avoided, as well.

If only she had noticed that Gaffney seemed restless. If only she had put more stock in the fact that Lions had never been known to be anything but flighty. What could she have prevented if she had paid more heed to the hemorrhaging of talented professionals on Gaffney and Lions' teams?

In short, when she ran the numbers, Limon realized that many highly talented individuals had been recruited and lost in recent years. The employee turnover in each office had been alarmingly high. Stevenson's age had become a concern, as well. At 69, he was long past the age where anyone but a workaholic would have entered retirement. And speaking of retirement, it occurred to Limon almost unexpectedly that she herself was 59.

Several terrifying questions hit her all at once:

1. How much of our success as a company depends on the level of talent we employ?
2. How will we replace all of these talented people?
3. If we don't replace them properly, can we survive?

TALENT IS IN SHORT SUPPLY

In current times, Diane Limon would not be alone in facing these fears. Her fears would only be compounded by the existing and future trends.

- In the coming fiscal year, it is estimated that 83 percent of current employees will be conducting active searches for new employment.
- In the coming fiscal year, some estimates show that approximately 493,000 people—31 percent of the federal workforce—will become eligible for retirement.

- By 2012, the 500 largest companies in the United States are expected to lose as much as 50 percent of their current leadership base.
- By 2015, the inventory of future leaders between the ages of 35 and 45 will decline by at least 15 percent.[4]

It can be disturbing to think about the prospect of replacing 83 percent of one's own employees. It might be harrowing to realize that 31 percent of the workforce is approaching the age of retirement. And it is especially so considering the fact that many of these 83 percent or 31 percent are highly talented individuals—the kinds of people that a company depends on to deliver high-quality products and services. What would it cost (in time, resources, and sheer monetary expense) to replace them?

Another problem exists. Not only are we likely to encounter the loss of many leaders in the coming months and years, but also we are also likely to experience a significant leadership shortage. Even today, nearly 70 percent of organizations are suffering from such shortages. And according to the U.S. Department of Education, 60 percent percent of new jobs will require skills that are possessed by only 20 percent of the current workforce.[5]

TROUBLE AHEAD

According to a Deloitte study, four particular industries will experience significant employee departure in the coming years: healthcare, manufacturing, energy, and the public sector. Consider the following statistics:

- The United States is expected to be 1 million nurses short of requirements by 2012.
- The National Association of Manufacturers claims that more than 80 percent of U.S. manufacturers will experience a shortage of skilled machinists and technicians.
- Per NASA, a mere 198,000 science and engineering graduates are expected to backfill up to 2 million retirements between 1998 and 2008.

Certainly, Human Capital Management has become a significant challenge for the vast majority of business executives. The problem is such that it can no longer be considered a specialized issue, one to hand off to the Human Resources department.[6] Senior leaders must take action now. The sooner, the better.

SEARCHING FOR ANSWERS

Diane Limon set out to do just that. Even before the unfavorable financials hit her desk, her goal was to determine what exactly was going on with her seemingly ailing company. Naturally, her first step was to call a meeting with each of the departments within Sky International. Her meeting with the Human Resources department proved particularly enlightening. What she found was that the people in HR followed a specific plan for hiring new high-level employees. In truth, Limon was quite impressed with the strategies outlined in these meetings.

When she presented the information to the other members of senior management, she discovered that she was not alone in this thinking. Everyone agreed: the current HR approach was not to blame. An effort was being made to attract top talent; the orientation programs were certainly efficient; employee morale seemed acceptable; high performers had been tagged for a sensible track of promotion.

So why was it that so many talented individuals seemed to be departing the company? And why was the HR department having such a hard time filling empty positions with the kinds of people who could improve company efficiency and profitability? There had to be something else going on . . .

EXAMINING HUMAN CAPITAL STRATEGIES

Diane Limon is not alone in another regard: She mistakenly believed that outdated Human Capital Management processes would continue to serve her company well in the changing business landscape. A poll of 307 business and government leaders in the United States—65 percent of whom reported to be in senior executive roles—shows that there are already Human Capital "solutions" in place at many corporations, both large and small.[7] The question remains, however, whether these "solutions" are satisfactory.

Of the respondents to the survey, a healthy 71 percent claimed to have succession planning (or some other process for maintaining leadership and critical talent) in place. To get to the bottom of whether these plans are effective, however, let's examine what motivated these 71 percent of respondents to implement a plan for Human Capital Management in the first place:

- 81 percent of respondents to the poll of 307 leaders recognized the need to develop internal bench strength.
- 74 percent suggested that their Human Capital plans focused on the need to develop individuals for likely future job vacancies.

- 47 percent saw succession planning and management as a useful retention tool.
- 35 percent pointed out the need to manage impending retirements.

So the problem is not that Human Capital plans do not exist in most organizations. Could it be that the plans are not comprehensive enough?

A majority of the 307 respondent organizations reported the use of six types of succession planning and management activities (as displayed in Figure 2.1). The two most frequent activities focused on the identification of high-potential employees (76 percent) and mission critical positions (71 percent). As far as identifying potential candidates for vacancies is concerned, one technique that is growing in frequency of use is that of talent inventories. It ranks third in this study, having been deployed by 65 percent of respondents.

If we delve deeper, the picture of where Sky International stands on these traditional plans looks muddy. As Limon would point out, Sky's HR department has been in the business of identifying high-potential people for more than ten years. But the HR people have certainly lacked qualified strategies for identifying individual contributors who can serve as a reservoir of talent and wisdom in the world of architecture. In other words, they jumped on the high-potential bandwagon long ago, but in the meantime, they haven't spent enough energy considering how to fill the slots for vice presidencies that are certain to open up in the near future. The people in HR have certainly done their jobs as prescribed, but they have not even begun to think about what a talent inventory will look like.

It seems likely, therefore, that the prescription is wrong. The effort is there; it just isn't complete.

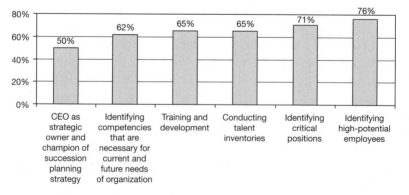

Figure 2.1
Succession Planning Activities Used Most Often

It is certainly not uncommon for an organization like Limon's to spend a great deal of time on one aspect of Human Capital Management and completely ignore another. In many cases, the CEO and other high-level leaders do not take enough responsibility for the process, either. For most organizations, the process that is most central to their future success—that of recruiting and maintaining highly talented individuals—simply does not cover every aspect of effective Human Capital Management.

CHANGING PERSPECTIVES

Diane Limon called a meeting with the rest of senior management. Surrounded by her peers, she expressed concern over the way Sky International was recruiting and retaining talented leaders and employees. She pointed out that there were several reasons why the company needed to realign its focus on Human Capital Management. The chief reason: if any of Sky's competitors decided to view Human Capital Management as a source of competitive advantage, they would begin poaching the most talented people. And without talented people to choose from, they would never be able to replace the aging leaders or shaky employees among them. The company would therefore suffer in the long term.

She presented evidence that she was not the only senior leader in the United States feeling this way. As she pointed out, she was just one leader among the two-thirds of organizations that considered Human Capital Management a source of competitive advantage.[8] She urged that CEOs of successful companies (those with higher than average return on assets) were twice as likely as CEOs of less successful companies to register alarm about the dwindling supply of talent coming up through the ranks.[9] And she reminded everyone present that there was simply no other way to explain the backsliding quarterly numbers.

Still, the other members of the board held their ground. Many pointed out that Human Capital Management strategies were already in place. Some claimed that the data about employee departure could not be trusted. Others failed to see the significance of a failure to promote from within.

But Limon fought her case. She explained that if the board continued to endorse inaction regarding the need to identify and prepare current and future leaders and highly talent performers, the risks would likely be dire. The company could not afford to lose Gaffney and Lions, but if it did, opportunities to attract new Gaffneys and Lions would be missed. Contracts increasingly would go to the competition. The most talented newcomers would continue their annual mass exodus. And given all of this, results were sure to fall desperately short of expectations in the years to come.

The worried CEO tried to paint the picture of a Sky International that suffered from a significant lack in leadership and talent. She tried to explain what it might be like to help run a company that was experiencing a deficit in the numbers necessary to rapidly seize, shape, and capitalize upon business growth opportunities. She tried to make everyone in the room visualize what it might be like to *watch somebody else* manage this disaster as they attempted to enjoy their retirement.

According to Limon, the outlook would be bleak. Sky would begin by losing city center projects in the big three cities. New York, Chicago, and Los Angeles would increasingly lean to the competition for its most artful and innovative projects. Her company, usually on the cutting edge of breakthroughs and disruptive strategies, would find itself playing catch-up to the chief competition in Seattle and San Diego for at least the next decade. Condos in new market spaces would spring up before Sky even had the time to realize that the market spaces existed. And at least one upstart architectural firm would make a splash in Cincinnati itself, leaving Sky with the prospect of doing battle on its own turf.

All of this would come to be simply because, in fewer than five years, Sky International would find itself run (at least in part) by people incapable or unwilling to execute new strategic initiatives, wisely guide new contracts, or realize targeted results. The company would suffer from a veritable void of strategic choices in the midst of ambiguous circumstances. In the end, if Sky was to face a decline from its pinnacle, it would not be because it did not have the capital or the marketing or the big name or the track record of success. It would be because the people running all facets of the firm would lack the vision it takes to make a company prosper over the competition.

Limon pleaded with the board to consider adopting a new strategy. She did all that she could to demonstrate that incomplete or misguided Human Capital strategies tend to lead to organizational breakdown. But in the end, she realized that she was fighting an uphill battle. As long as the board believed that the company had effective Human Capital practices in place, she would never be able to win them over.

THE HUMAN CAPITAL CYCLE

Limon's challenge is now clear: she must make the board see the light. She must make them understand that, just as with marketing and sales and R&D, Human Capital Management is an issue that senior management must address personally.

Despite her research and her meetings and her reassurances from HR, Limon cannot feel satisfied with a system that does not seem to be producing the results she desires. As she now considers this to be a core business issue, she understands that there is a compelling need for a broader, more systemic, and comprehensive approach than the one her company currently employs. She has found the solution to her company's otherwise inexplicable first quarter losses: while sales and research and organizational efficiency are certainly important, superior corporate performance goes hand in hand with a focus on Human Capital Management.

In squaring off with the board, Limon faced only one true obstacle—one that she seemed to come back to again and again, regardless how hard she fought for her perspective: she needed a definable process that she could use to illustrate her point. She needed a Human Capital process comprehensive and powerful enough to handle the ever-changing needs of her expanding company. She needed the Human Capital Cycle.

SUMMARY

By now, it should be apparent that even with detailed research and excellent intentions, traditional methods of Human Capital Management tend to be too one-dimensional. Companies focus on one discipline while other important disciplines go untended—and, as a result, key employees wind up slipping through the cracks.

The truth remains that Human Capital Management is perhaps the most significant focus a company's leadership can undertake. Studies show a 90 percent increase in shareholder value for organizations that focus on Human Capital Management.[10]

As you will see in the pages to come, it was only through a deliberate focus on Human Capital Management that Limon managed to overcome her company's financial shortfalls and develop a deep leadership and talent benchmark for the future. With the Human Capital Cycle in place, Sky International would find itself more capable of seizing and capitalizing upon spontaneous opportunities, realizing strategic targets, and rising to the toughest challenges. Their success certainly is not specialized. Any company that redirects its focus on Human Capital will realize tremendous results. Any company that adopts the Human Capital Cycle will experience the Triple Win.

3

INTRODUCTION TO THE HUMAN CAPITAL CYCLE

CEO DIANE LIMON knew that her firm's Human Capital Management strategy was not working. Even if numbers could be cited to suggest that employee talent was being managed in some form or another, she could see that, unless changes were made immediately, the near future would bring the potential for a disastrous shortfall in talented individuals.

Somehow, some way, Limon had to convince the rest of the board that Human Resources matters were no longer so specialized. She needed to make the point that, while high employee turnover was not currently affecting the company's productivity, market advantage, and creativity, it was bound to have a detrimental effect on its ability to approach all facets of the architecture market in the near term. Without changes to the Human Capital approach, money and market share would be lost to the competition.

The problem as Limon saw it lay in the fact that not every employee or prospective employee follows a predictable, linear path when it comes to their career or professional goals. Not everyone is willing or able to take an entry-level position, work hard and smart, wait for that big promotion, and then start the process all over again. In fact, data suggest that very few people even stay with a single company for their entire working lives any more. And there simply are not enough individuals coming up through the ranks who are ready or able to excel within the many upper management and other leadership positions due to open up in the coming years.

Organizations are constantly in flux, as well. It becomes nearly impossible to insert all the proper employees into a given position and expect them to flourish. Even more trying is the task of assessing internal talent and then implementing that talent at the right company levels. But the most difficult undertaking of all is keeping everyone happy—high performers must be afforded a career track that they deem acceptable and low performers must be trained or reassigned to areas where they might realize greater motivation or productivity.

All of this might sound chaotic. It certainly can be. It is for this exact reason that traditional approaches to Human Capital Management—all those approaches that preach the importance of keeping prospects, new recruits, and existing employees on a straight, predefined track—simply do not work as effectively as they once did. With an effective organizational strategy, and with the right process in place, the chaos can be averted—and all Human Capital shortfalls can be overcome. The immediate result: better and more talented people working for the organization. The result of these people: higher quality products and services. The ultimate result: most satisfied customers, happier employees, and a healthier bottom line for the organization.

A MORE DYNAMIC APPROACH

In the pages to come, you will find a far more effective alternative to the traditionally simplistic model of employee recruitment, training, promotion, and retention—an alternative that many senior executives have come to embrace. This broader and more systematic approach to Human Capital Management is known as the Human Capital Cycle. It is a practical model that encompasses a range of strategic and tactical considerations required to more fully address core business issues and effects on all three elements to company success: customers, organizations, and their employees (or what we call the Triple Win).

Simply put, the Human Capital Cycle tends to lead to a Triple Win because it is more dynamic, more comprehensive, and strategically significant than today's typically narrow definition of talent management. It does not call for the confinement to the Human Resources department the responsibility for attracting, developing, and retaining key people. This is no linear approach. It is a cycle based exclusively on the concept of system dynamics, and as such, it is comprehensive, resourceful, and adaptable to all needs—however specialized —related to activating business strategies and achieving better results from an organization's workforce.

Now, the term "system dynamics" typically leads to visions of complex mathematical equations. It conjures up images of mathematicians crunching numbers in labs at the Massachusetts Institute of Technology (MIT)—and for good reason: the fundamentals of system dynamics were first developed by Jay Forrester in the 1950s at MIT. System dynamics is certainly a complicated matter, but for simplicity's sake, we will bypass concepts such as higher order and differential equations and get right down to how it relates to Human Capital Management.

In short, the Human Capital needs of organizations that operate in today's unpredictable marketplace are broader than they used to be. The most successful

Human Capital plans must address interdisciplinary systems such as cognitive and social psychology, economics, and related social sciences.

Traditional models of Human Capital Management approach the marketplace as if recruiting, training, and retaining employees is a static issue. In other words, they assume an inaccurate and highly unlikely representation of reality. For example, it would be ridiculous for Limon to approach the predicament regarding her drastically understaffed pool of draftsmen and draftswomen by telling Sky's Human Resources department to expend all their efforts on hiring as many new and talented draftsmen and draftswomen as possible. Why? Because while attention is being paid fully to one problem, other problems may arise. Employee orientation might suffer. Talented staff already on the payroll may become disgruntled if they get passed over for an open position. And recruitment in other areas of the firm would surely be sacrificed.

Human Capital Management, at its base, is a series of situations and goals. As system dynamics tells us, the trouble with situations and goals is that they do not always fall into a clean separation of problem, decision, and results. Instead, they operate like a system involving a group of interrelated, interdependent elements that form a complex whole. As they come together, they tend to interact with one another. And this interaction is not always so orderly. When one solution is implemented in the hopes of resolving a problematic situation—say, Limon's draftsmen and draftswomen issue—new (and potentially problematic) situations are created. This of course sets up the need for a *new* assessment and *another* decision, and so on.

With the proper system in place, Human Capital Management does not need to be as difficult or even as chaotic. To attack a broad and fluctuating problem, one must work to implement a broad and fluctuating system—one that operates less like a straight path and more like a cycle with various interchangeable phases, all of them interacting with one another on a given organizational issue, all of them pushing each other toward the same ultimate goal.

THE HUMAN CAPITAL CYCLE: AN ADAPTABLE SYSTEM

The Human Capital Cycle connects all facets of Human Capital Management in a more appropriate way. In so doing, it contains the tools necessary for an executive to vigilantly monitor the Human Capital landscape for any potential consequences to customers, the organization, or any pockets of employees. It adapts to any and all unforeseen problems and new factors that may spring up. It is designed for ease of use over the long term. Most importantly, it leads directly to the Triple Win, which is something that any organization can identify with.

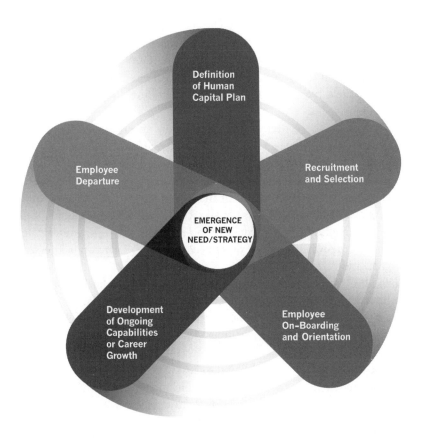

The diagram above illustrates that the ultimate goals of the Human Capital Cycle depend equally on the performance of six component parts. Each component part should be considered an individual stage in the employee lifecycle. As a whole, the cycle is the confluence of these six stages. It represents a complete, synchronized assembly that sets in motion the full range of organizational Human Capital.

The six stages of the Human Capital Cycle are identified as follows:

1. Emergence of New Need/Strategy
2. Definition of Human Capital Plan

3.   Recruitment and Selection
4.   Employee On-Boarding and Orientation
5.   Development of Ongoing Capabilities or Career Growth
6.   Employee Departure.

One thing you will notice about the Human Capital Cycle figure is the phase in the center. The emergence of new need or strategy is quite simply the foundation of the Human Capital Cycle. As such, it can be considered the most important phase in the process. Without it, the others become irrelevant, and top organizations may continue to follow their linear approach to Human Capital Management.

This phase at the center of the illustration encompasses the changing dynamics of today's business world. It highlights the latest demands, strictures, and trends of the organization, the marketplace in which it operates, and the labor market from which it draws employees. It perpetually scans both the internal and external environment of the organization that sets it in motion. It is sensitized to analyze evidence of all factors that influence mission critical success. And finally, it seeks to identify the emergence of new, strategic needs and points to the ways in which those needs may be effectively addressed by the organization's Human Capital.

Now, all of that considered, each of the six stages of the Human Capital Cycle finds its own unique importance. Each is characterized by its own set of key tasks, desirable outcomes, issues or questions to address, and likely consequences if the efforts are left incomplete or are completed in an unsuccessful way.

In the chapters that follow, each of the six stages of the Human Capital Cycle will be explored in greater depth. The desirable outcomes will be identified; and their respective importance to the Triple Win outcome will be revealed. You will find best practices and recommendations for success. Throughout the process, we will continue to follow the story of Sky International, and in addition, several other organizational examples will be provided in order to illustrate key points.

Our intent is to provide a practical, holistic, systemic view of the Human Capital Cycle and the principal tasks, outcomes, and questions to be addressed during each stage. You will not find reference to the traditional processes, systems, policies, and practices of the typical human resource function. Nor will you find an endorsement or pitch for a specific software system or other enabling product. We aim only to provide the strategic direction necessary to optimally engage your organization's Human Capital, thereby improving your competitive advantage and steering you closer to that ultimate Triple Win.

A NEW RESPONSIBILITY

As Limon so appropriately demonstrates, Human Capital Management is no longer a Human Resources issue. This issue belongs to every member of the senior management team. The cycle illustrated earlier not only presumes that senior management will be actively involved in implementing the strategy, but also it *depends* on their leadership and accountability. This is simply because a dynamic mind is needed to implement a dynamic system that operates within a dynamic environment.

Moving forward, we must take into account the fact that the labor market is unstable, or at the very least, unpredictable. It does not always align with the needs of organizations, nor does it function with the level of stability or flexibility required to easily meet the needs of *all* organizations that draw upon it. The few organizations that appropriately capitalize on identifying, deploying, developing, propagating, and protecting their existing and prospective talent base will find *significant* competitive advantage.

Talented individuals have become the most precious and scarce resource in modern business. For those who would embrace the need to approach this resource as a strategically advantageous commodity, the Human Capital Cycle provides a new path, one that will achieve a far greater return on organizational success.

Chapter

4

EMERGENCE OF NEW
NEED/STRATEGY

A LL GREAT BUSINESS STRATEGIES rely upon a central, driving element
to bring the whole operation to fruition. A company that hopes to expand its
customer base might put its faith in a targeted marketing campaign, for
example. Likewise, an organization looking to improve profit margins might
search for ways to cut production costs. When it comes to the Human Capital
Cycle, the central, driving element is clear: new organizational strategies are
just as dependent on successful Human Capital Management initiatives as they
are on marketing, sales, or R&D agendas (or any other business discipline, for
that matter).

Put simply: a business strategy is only as good as the people who implement
it. Better people—those employees who are most committed and prepared to
help implement the strategy—*always* lead to greater success.

The Human Capital Cycle is certainly not the only Human Capital
Management strategy in practice today. What separates the Human Capital
Cycle from all the others, however, is that it is the only approach that properly
recognizes that central, driving element: the direct correlation between Human
Capital Management success and *business* success. In other words, this cycle
recognizes that Human Capital Management should not be considered a matter
best left to the HR department—not when there is so much revenue, market
share, and favorable public perception to be gained or lost.

In today's rapidly expanding and evolving marketplace, if a company ignores
its Human Capital Management needs when crafting new organizational
strategy, the consequences can be dire—consequences that are likely to be felt
by the organization, its customers, and its employees alike. The company will
fall short of its desired outcomes, experiencing untimely and often disappointing results. More importantly, without motivated, knowledgeable, and capable
people in place, it will have wasted resources, time, and money on an
underutilized strategy.

For this reason, organizations simply cannot afford to isolate Human
Capital Management from other business issues. In order to realize the greatest

measure of success in any strategy, the senior management team must take a proactive approach to the consideration and implementation of the Human Capital Cycle.

PUTTING PEOPLE FIRST

James Copeland is the head of a cutting-edge green electricity company known as Solar Electric, Inc., though if you asked him, he might tell you that he isn't sure why he managed to keep his job. He is living testament to the importance of senior management taking charge of an organization's Human Capital Management initiatives. As Copeland would say, "When you think of your business strategy, you have to think of your people first."

Before the downturn, Solar Electric enjoyed modest business results that were only getting better due to the recent uptick in customer demand for green power. Of course, the company was not without the occasional customer complaint (especially as it ironed out its initial supply issues and power shortfalls), but that could only be expected.

But just as Solar Electric seemed to reach that critical mass where it could properly meet its supply needs, just when everything seemed to be going Copeland's way, the complaints began to grow more frequent. Without warning, customer satisfaction had dipped measurably. Worse yet, new regulations on the nation's power infrastructure were implemented by the government, effectively paving the way for more competition to enter the fray. What this meant was that a wind power corporation known as Wind Initiative was now free to begin bidding on contracts and scooping up market share.

In response to these impending disasters, Copeland called for a company-wide efficiency study. The results were less than stellar. The unfavorable findings revealed by the study were bad enough, but adding insult to injury, Copeland also made the mistake of publishing said findings.

The resultant public outcry could not have been more damaging. The glare of public scrutiny produced significant discomfort in the board room as well as on Main Street. Tension began to mount within the community, as many customers openly voiced concerns about their rates of service, already far higher than they had been promised (and rising all the time). Thousands threatened to switch back to natural gas—or worse yet, over to Wind Initiative—a move that would rock Solar Electric's profitability outlook. Meanwhile, most of the company's own employees expressed concern about job security.

The senior management team had been wholly unprepared for such a disastrous set of findings. Unrest erupted among their ranks, as many found difficulty even conducting civil discussions about the boundaries of their authority. None truly knew the expectations for their actions in response to the published study. And ultimately, all were at a loss as to what to do about the tremendous sag in public opinion.

Copeland's first instinct was to blame himself. In his mind, each of these separate disasters could be traced to his decision to run and publish the study in the first place. But in time, he came to realize that this line of thinking was far too simplistic. After all, there were certainly other factors at play. For one, the market landscape had been suddenly and drastically altered by new rules laid down by the government (and few can prepare for such a dramatic shift in the playing field).

In what can only be called sheer desperation (since, at the time, it was considered by many key executives at the firm as a last resort effort) Solar Electric decided to explore new Human Capital Management strategies in the hopes that they might help alleviate some of the pressure on all facets of the company. When Copeland began to examine the operations of his employees, what he found was eye-opening, to say the least. Inadequate communications abound throughout the organization. Hostility seemed to run rampant within the ranks of the senior management (not surprising, given that the company had undergone several reorganizations of management over the preceding several years). There seemed to be too much focus by management on daily operations and not enough on the big picture. On the employee level, poor practices had drained away morale over the long term. And there was evidence of low accountability for standards of performance, a lack of trust, competing interests, and even a reduction in the strength of employee knowledge in managing the business and providing customer service.

At its face, one might examine this story about Solar Electric and simply decide that this bleak picture of Human Capital and company outlook can be chalked up to poor leadership on the part of senior management. But as Copeland came to discover, the trouble was not a lack of leadership, but a lack of *appropriately focused* leadership. Simply put, the company was not failing because of poor strategies. It wasn't even failing because of the published study. It was failing because it never took the time to align its strategies with its Human Capital concerns. And as a result, it found itself mired in declining public opinion and tense employee relations.

For Solar Electric, the day it first decided to undertake a revision of its Human Capital plan was the day that it began to turn itself around. The trek back from this seriously distasteful set of consequences would be a slow one; one that would require radical changes in the philosophy, policies, processes, and behaviors in virtually every corner of Solar Electric's Human Capital initiative. But over time, signals of a potential Triple Win would begin to show themselves on the horizon.

Now that the new Human Capital initiative is in place and running, the task of recruiting the right people, keeping them happy, and ensuring that they are contributing to business success has become almost second nature for Solar Electric. Today, Copeland realizes that his company's apparent rebound can be attributed to a single philosophical change: to keep all new organizational needs working in tandem with Human Capital concerns. And he's now a whole lot more confident about the prospects of keeping his job.

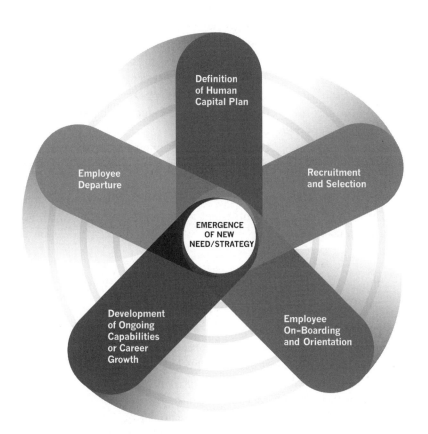

The illustration should make one thing abundantly clear: while its stages are both independent and interdependent, the Human Capital Cycle simply cannot function without this central, driving stage. The emergence of new strategy serves as the genesis, the initiating source of motion, and the driver of the six-stage cycle.

THE EMERGENCE OF NEW NEED/STRATEGY STAGE: MISSION CRITICAL FACTORS

There are many factors that contribute to success at this particular stage of the Human Capital Cycle. Those organizations that perform exceptionally well tend to have in place a set of mission critical factors that directly relate to the health and vitality of their business. These mission critical factors may include:

- A thorough knowledge of the most important (and perhaps scarcest) sources of value to the organization and its customers
- Knowledge of where the company stands in the marketplace
- An understanding of the company's unique economic footprint
- A collection of appropriate organizational data
- The determination of the profile of the company's ideal customers
- A full stream of current and future products and services that produce prime revenue sources
- An understanding of the company's premium regulatory domains, as well as its best opportunities for current success, future growth, and long-term financial viability
- Measures to protect all trade secrets and/or intellectual property
- The critical knowledge and talent necessary to steward all of the above qualifications.

GOALS AND OUTCOMES

For those who do not believe that a new corporate and Human Capital strategy is necessary, consider a report published by The Economist Intelligence Unit entitled *CEO Briefing: Corporate Priorities for 2006 and Beyond*.[1] As this report suggests, in the years leading up to 2010, global organizations should be keenly aware four emerging factors expected to influence success. Not coincidentally, all of them relate to Human Capital needs. First, forecasters believe that it will become increasingly difficult to meet customer and market needs in new areas, particularly in developing markets. As business becomes more and more global, the task of managing employees from even greater distances (and through differing cultures and languages) will become a reality for many more companies. In this highly fluid, global economy, talent will be scarcer and more difficult to find. And finally, it is important to realize that all business and

Human Capital decisions will have to be sound, given that it will be far more difficult to compete effectively in this rapidly changing environment.

This driving stage of the Human Capital Cycle recognizes and provides measures against these potentially damaging scenarios. In order to overcome such future difficulty, it is important that a company embrace the following list of goals, integrating them into its own emerging new strategy.

UNCOVER ORGANIZATIONAL NEED AND DESIRED OUTCOMES

The first goal in any new strategy should be an obvious one. A company cannot know where it intends to go until it takes measures to discover how it can be improved internally. No organization is perfect. All could use improvements in the hopes of gaining more market share and securing for the future. James Copeland achieved this primary goal by conducting a company-wide survey. But he ran into trouble initially because his survey did not include the most important aspect to consider when crafting new strategy: Human Capital needs. While it is true that all surveys conducted must focus on the productivity, performance, and capability of the company, they must focus at least as much attention on the *people* who drive that productivity, performance, and capability, as well.

DETERMINE OVERARCHING STRATEGY TO ACHIEVE OUTCOMES

Once the survey data is in place, the senior management team may use what it has learned to begin crafting strategies to achieve the desired outcomes. As with the survey, however, it is important to include Human Capital concerns in any and all discussions. A strategy is only as good as the people who execute it, after all.

DEVELOP A COMPREHENSIVE, INTEGRATED, AND SYSTEMATIC APPROACH TO EXECUTING THE STRATEGY

This goal is absolutely critical. It is key to the success of any operation. It is one thing to recognize the need for a new strategy. And it is certainly no easy task determining how and when to execute that strategy. But if the strategy itself does not include a comprehensive approach to engaging the right people, ensuring productivity, overcoming obstacles, and reaching given milestones, then it is likely to achieve less desirable results.

The Human Capital Cycle is particularly dynamic because it is itself a comprehensive, integrated, and systematic approach—one that fits in with any traditional business strategies crafted by the executive suite. More than anything, the act of exacting new strategy takes talented people. And as a model, the cycle is ideal for the task of recruiting, training, and ensuring the continuing success of the most talented people for the job.

CRAFT A THOROUGH ACTION PLAN, COMPLETE WITH APPROPRIATE ACCOUNTABILITIES FOR RESULTS

Consider this the road map of the new strategy. Before any journey can begin, it is absolutely critical that the company knows exactly where it is going— and more importantly, how to get there.

SET PERFORMANCE MILESTONES TO MEASURE PROGRESS

This goal might seem obvious, but it is nevertheless of critical importance. Performance milestones serve a dual purpose. First, they help to keep morale high—it is far easier for a person (regardless of which level of the company that person falls into) to remain committed to a task, if that person can see measurable results, after all. Second, they demonstrate to the executive team whether or not the strategy was a good one to begin with. If milestones are being met, then the strategy can and should continue. If not, then the company should consider revising the strategy.

Successful organizations tend to set this evaluation process before they implement the strategy and even craft the execution plan. Periodic evaluation not only ensures that the Human Capital related to the strategy is being properly managed, but it allows for a greater sense of adaptability for the plan, as well. If you know where you are performing or underperforming, it is far easier to make mid-stream adjustments and corrections in order to get the most out of your committed resources.

PLEDGE ORGANIZATIONAL COMMITMENT TO FOLLOW THROUGH WITH THE STRATEGY

With the strategy now mapped out, the next logical step is commitment. Strategies that have only partial commitment from the senior management team tend to be misguided and uneven. More often than not, one or more aspects of the strategy fall short, causing the entire operation to fail or underperform. For this reason, before beginning any strategy, it is important that the company ensure commitment from the entire team.

DEFINE THE SPECIFIC NEEDS RELATED TO HUMAN CAPITAL

This outcome is what separates the Human Capital Cycle from all other Human Capital strategies—it dares to include Human Capital measures in *all* business strategies. There is good reason for this: It is one thing to have a detailed road map in place, but that road map isn't useful unless the company has the right people to drive the route. Too many organizations make decisions on new corporate strategy and then simply leave the hiring needs to the HR department. This common action leads to far too many strategies falling short of desired goals. As the Human Capital Cycle demonstrates, Human Capital needs *are* business needs. In fact, they are certainly the most critical business needs. It has been said before, but it bears repeating: a business strategy is only as good as the people who perform it.

Some strategies require a bigger or more specialized sales team. Some strategies require the expansion or contraction of skilled laborers. Still others call for the increase in talent and knowledge within a given business discipline. Regardless of what the strategy calls for, it is important that the senior management team take the time to determine the exact characteristics of the person ideally suited to carry out all levels of that strategy.

The result of this outcome should be a detailed list of roles that the strategy depends on. Each role should be matched with the definition of the ideal person to fill that role. This is not simply a wish list, however. The focal point for any such outcome must be the availability and readiness of all talented and knowledgeable personnel. A company cannot seek what is not available to it, after all.

ALIGN THE STRATEGY WITH THE EMPLOYEE VALUE PROPOSITION

In keeping with the theme that a strategy is only as successful as its people are talented, this final goal is easily the most essential to the process. The Employee Value Proposition (EVP) is so important to any given strategy because it answers a key question for current and future employees: Why would a promising leader want to grow, develop, and contribute to this organization and this strategy over the long term? Simply put, it is the *branding* of the employment experience—a brand that each employee should realize not just at the orientation stage, but throughout his/her entire career in that organization.

The Employee Value Proposition focuses on those distinctive characteristics or experiences that set the company in question aside from other employment situations. Ideally, the EVP promotes clear appeal to those who possess the critical knowledge and talent that is essential to the Triple Win.

When constructing an EVP, it is important to make connections to factors that appeal most to the desirable prospective employee (all those people most apt to help the company achieve its latest strategies). For a few examples of these appealing factors, note the report conducted by *The Conference Board,* wherein employees were asked what they wanted most or expected from their employers.[2] Their top three responses were:

1. Growth and development opportunities
2. An environment of open communications
3. Work that is challenging and interesting.

The most successful organizations create their Employee Value Proposition with as much vigor as they create their Customer Value Proposition. These organizations realize that engaged employees stimulate engaged customers. They spend a significant amount of effort and attention on adhering to the Customer Value Proposition, but that effort and attention is mirrored against the Employee Value Proposition—and carried throughout the entire Human Capital Cycle.

WHY HUMAN CAPITAL *MATTERS*

If it is not abundantly clear that a strategy is only as good as the talented people behind it, then consider the following statistics. What you will find is twofold: First, most companies simply are not paying enough attention to Human Capital needs. And second, the companies that *do* pay attention find opportunities to gain *significant* leverage over the competition.

From a study conducted by *The Economist*'s Intelligence Unit and Deloitte:

- 88 percent of respondents noted that people issues will become vital to business success in the next two to five years

- 77 percent reported that the Human Resources function itself does not play a critical enough role in the strategic agenda of their organization (or in the pursuit of desired business results).[3]

From research published in *The McKinsey Quarterly* (surveying 29 multinational organizations from a range of industries):

- Nearly 50 percent of respondents expressed concern about the alignment of Human Capital or talent strategies within the business; one Human Resource executive went so far as to describe this shortfall as a significant blind spot for all executives
- 54 percent of respondents indicated that senior executives or managers do not spend sufficient time on management of talent
- 52 percent perceived this low level of commitment to talent development as a substantial barrier to their success.[4]

On a more macro scale, in April 2007, the U.S. Department of Commerce advisory committee on Measuring Innovation in the 21st Century issued a public request for comment as part of its strategy to develop a set of metrics to assess the state of innovation within the U.S. economy. A committee member, Don Siegel, professor and associate dean of the Anderson Graduate School of Management at the University of California–Riverside, noted that the United States is stuck in an older, industrial mindset even though it has shifted to become much more focused on knowledge. The old system of measures for labor continues to be our primary area of focus.[5]

On the other hand, the CFO of Wells Fargo has been extending metrics into areas beyond traditional financial measures. He counts team-member engagement as one such measure, even though it doesn't show up on the general ledger. He has observed that those people who have higher scores in employee engagement have also ranked higher in both productivity and customer satisfaction.[6]

Similarly, Best Buy found a direct correlation between employee engagement scores and increases in store operating income. Every tenth of a point in engagement scores was equated with $100,000 in store results.[7] For the Hilton Corporation, a 5 percent rise in customer retention rates is connected to a 1.1 percent increase in revenue within the following year.[8]

The lesson here should be clear: Organizations cannot afford to isolate Human Capital Management from business issues and strategies.

THE COMPONENTS OF A SUCCESSFUL STRATEGY

Each of the goals listed in the previous section is critically important to the success of any new strategy. We have found in our research that successful organizations are so successful because they tend to have processes in place to educate, organize, and engage people who serve as sentinels to oversee company accountability and search for new phenomena that might lead to a disruption of these mission critical factors. When a shift is detected—and it is determined that management must be alerted—the findings are quickly delivered to the attention of at least one member of the executive or C-suite (chief officers). If further verification is warranted, the evidence is typically brought to the full executive membership for affirmation and formulation of the appropriate strategy. Human Capital considerations are always included in this process.

The essential component of this process—and the Human Capital Cycle that supports it—is that it is not based on a linear mode of thinking. Rather, it is rooted in System Dynamics. System Dynamics is obviously a broad topic, but here we refer to it only in the sense that the Human Capital Cycle, as well as all the best business strategies, is a system that rotates and operates in flux. It is one that adapts to its constantly changing environment; one that relies on its component parts, but is not critically dependent on them.

In summary, the System Dynamics of the Human Capital Cycle features two important things to consider. First, the cycle is and should always be integrated with all other business strategies. Second, it comes equipped with a feedback process designed to keep all members of the senior management team informed about how the cycle and its integrated strategies are performing. This feedback process is known as the double-loop feedback stream.

The double-loop feedback stream is certainly not as complicated as it sounds. And while it is certainly cyclical in nature, it is simpler to understand when broken down into steps.

As Figure 4.1 demonstrates, the double-loop feedback stream begins with senior management relaying the initial message about the strategy or its directives to all those employees designated to carry out that strategy or directive. It is followed by specific questions from the employees to senior management. Senior management then provides clarification for those questions, an act that completes the first "loop" in the stream. The second loop often begins once the employees have put the strategy or directive in motion—as it features new questions about the strategy or directive on the part of the employees. The second loop is then closed when senior management provides further clarity or confirmation to the latest round of questions.

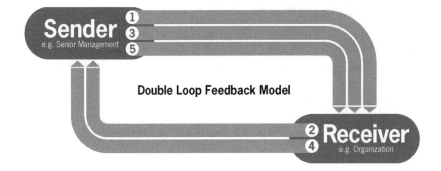

Double Loop Feedback Model

Figure 4.1
Double-Loop Feedback Stream

Of course, the double-loop feedback stream is never truly "closed." It should be considered a continuous process that has been integrated into the Human Capital Cycle and the new strategies that it supports. It is an essential component to strategy execution.

BEST PRACTICES FOR EXECUTING A NEW STRATEGY

For the average company, when implementing a new strategy, as much as 37 percent of the potential value of that strategy is lost.[9] With so much value being lost, it is absolutely *essential* to construct a comprehensive, integrated, and systemic approach to the execution of the given strategy. Without such an initiative, even with good intentions in place, many companies will fall short of their strategic goals.

Further study shows that, more often than not, this shortfall in value can be attributed to three factors related to Human Capital Management:

- Performance management systems are often left out of sync with the implemented strategy. This accounts for nearly 40 percent of the total shortfall.
- Many times, companies fail to allocate the appropriate level of resources to the strategy. This accounts for 30 percent of the total shortfall.
- Perhaps most startling is the fact that many organizations fail to engage in the changes required to execute the strategy successfully. This accounts for more than 20 percent of the total shortfall.

EXECUTING A NEW STRATEGY IN ACTION

Unlike James Copeland at Solar Electric, Bill Johns realized in the early going that the announcement of new regulatory governance for the energy sector was going to mean vast changes in the rules for his company's environment. Chairman of Wind Initiative, Johns understood that if his company was to continue its rise in market share, it would have to take advantage of as many of these new markets as it possibly could. So, to that end, he engaged the entire organization to the act of affirming the full effect of these substantial regulatory changes on the company itself, its market space, its existing customer base, and its employees.

In keeping with the goals and outcomes of any successful new strategy, the senior management team at Wind Initiative promptly organized to determine what the new governmental regulations meant for them. In short, they determined that they would be able to leverage all this new government funding to gain substantial market share on their state's green-minded energy consumers. With 10 percent of the state's consumers currently using green power, and 8 percent of the state's consumers getting that green power from Solar Electric, it seemed to the executives at Wind Initiative that there was plenty of room to grow—especially given the fact that studies showed an increase in demand for green power growing at nearly 200 percent per year.

It was determined that the overarching strategy to gaining more market share would be to conduct a targeted marketing campaign that focused primarily on new green-power customers and secondarily on existing green-power customers. Johns and the rest of senior management realized that even a nominal effort in gathering market share from Solar Electric would be effective for two reasons. First, Wind Initiative could offer energy prices far more attractive than its competitor. Second, Solar Electric was not exactly enjoying record ratings in customer satisfaction. In the end, it was determined that a successful marketing campaign might help Wind Initiative to grow by as much as 100 percent in the first year alone.

The board would later reconvene to determine a full set of analytics that would drive the strategy forward and help them achieve their substantial growth goal. They established the probability for risk (how much marketing time could they afford before they cut too far into their operating budget, impeding their ability to add more wind generators and thus grow their power output capability?). They surveyed their customer base to determine the most desirable characteristics of their product. And they surveyed their employees to determine the areas of the company they needed to improve or expand upon (one determination was that they would need far more technicians if they were to achieve the substantial expansion they aimed for).

The steps to achieving the company's goal were laid out and the action plan blueprinted. Performance milestones (such as 50 percent growth in the first quarter) were established. And every member of the senior management team pledged commitment to the plan.

But the most important finding during this strategy formulation came in the form of Human Capital concerns. Despite the fact that he had been committed to Human Capital needs from the very beginning of the strategy, it came as quite a surprise to Johns. The board realized that they needed to examine the degree of leadership bench strength within the company itself. There were just so many key players in upper management that were already within the window of eligibility for retirement. This was particularly problematic, given that it was quickly determined that, in order for Wind Initiative to respond favorably to the regulatory shift proposed by the government, they would need to maintain an acceptable level of stability, critical knowledge, talent, and experience in their leadership bench over a longer period of time.

So the natural action was obvious: Wind Initiative needed to establish a deeper bench immediately—one with a new set of capabilities that could deal effectively with the changes in the regulatory environment.

Returning to the probable scenarios that could unfold over the coming decade, selected members of senior management led group discussions to identify the full range of critical knowledge, skills, experience, and talent required to perform effectively in the new market space. The definitions of this critical knowledge and talent were then used as a kind of filter for crafting an effective company-wide census.

As a result of the census, Wind Initiative learned a number of things about its employees. First, it learned that only a smaller percentage than expected of its employees demonstrated the right combination of critical knowledge and talent to succeed in the new market space. Second, the census also determined exactly which people were already effectively demonstrating those skills. Of these talented people, it demonstrated which of them were ready for movement into new or replacement positions. From the rest, the census highlighted which people most needed some level of developmental experience (and why). Third, the census revealed exactly how many additional people would be required to fulfill the strategy (and more importantly, the appropriate level of experience and expertise needed in each individual role).

Wind Initiative's senior management then set to work on assembling a flexible bench for both the near and longer term leadership and critical talent performer roles. A fair and equitable process was created to ensure the right types of development, ongoing review of candidate strengths and readiness, and the actual application of the bench strength plan when new opportunities occurred.

A double-loop feedback stream was created to deliver clear messages and statements of intent to all interested audiences. This feedback stream ensured that everyone knew their roles and expectations while simultaneously ensuring that the bench strength process was effectively fulfilling the Human Capital needs over the long term. It also helped to monitor the situation and make prompt adjustments.

Wind Initiative is an excellent example of an organization that took overt action to ensure that their critical knowledge performers, talented individuals, and leadership base were in alignment with the near and long-term needs of the business. The results of this strategy were staggering. While Wind Initiative did not gain as much of Solar Electric's existing customers as it had anticipated, its systematic approach to its strategy—and, more importantly, the Human Capital needed to exact that strategy—led to incredible growth in the company and a much more competitive position in the new market space. Revenues climbed, more and more employees began expressing happiness in their roles and contentment in their futures with the company, and the customers expressed satisfaction far higher than with that of the competition. Truly, Wind Initiative had achieved a Triple Win.

SUMMARY

It should be clear by now that all great strategies are both comprehensive and adaptable. The comprehensiveness of this strategy definition should include the steps necessary to achieving all goals and outcomes. It should outline a detailed action plan and include a set of specific performance milestones. It is important that it takes into consideration all risks and steps to mitigate those risks. It should feature a powerful feedback stream to help keep it running efficiently and effectively. It cannot be set in motion until all members of senior management pledge their commitment to it. But most importantly, it must be carried out by the most appropriate and talented individuals possible.

All new strategies require a detailed examination of Human Capital concerns. Aligning the strategy with the Employee Value Proposition is only the beginning of that examination. The senior management team must take steps to integrate the company's Human Capital needs with each of its interdependent business strategies. The best (and perhaps the only effective) way to do this is to incorporate a Human Capital strategy that is every bit as dynamic and adaptable as a successful business strategy must be. That strategy is the Human Capital Cycle.

With the new strategy identified and defined, the driving stage of the cycle is now in place. Senior management may now move on to building the rest of the Human Capital framework around this central strategy. The result will be a system that sustains and adapts itself more easily—and one that lends a great deal to employee, customer, and company success. Truly, the Human Capital Cycle is the source of the Triple Win.

Chapter

5

DEFINITION OF THE HUMAN CAPITAL PLAN

I T IS CLEAR THAT having better, more talented people leads to higher revenues, decreased expenses, improved market share, and heightened public opinion. It is the crux of the Triple Win: that an organization with a high percentage of talented people tends to experience improved value for the customer, the organization, and the employees themselves. To meet these common business strategies, many organizations have already begun an examination of new Human Capital Management measures. So what's next?

Like all business projects, implementing the Human Capital Cycle begins with defining organizational needs. During this definition stage, all members of senior management should plan to determine exactly what kinds of talented people they will need in order to deliver the Triple Win. They will determine the talent, competencies, knowledge, skills, abilities, and motivations that are required for superior performance—and then use that skill-set as an evaluation measure of all current, potential, and future employees.

Given that it sets the foundation for future decisions on the people hired, trained, and fostered by the company, the definition stage is perhaps the most important stage of the Human Capital Plan. Unfortunately, according to recent data, it also seems to be the stage that most executives tend to ignore.[1]

This is a troubling trend. Not only does it mean that too many organizations fail to see the direct correlation between talent levels and business success, but also it means that most Human Capital programs lack direction. For any organization, such a lack of direction can lead to a number of consequences (i.e. an underperforming Human Capital program, a lack of organizational fairness in the eyes of employees, an inability to put the right people with the right skills in the right places at the right time, a Human Resources team that too often misses the mark on its functional support, etc.). Over the long term, all of these consequences have the tendency to contribute to a decline in an organization's ability to meet its business goals.

From a market share perspective, it is also an encouraging trend. If the majority of organizations are not paying proper attention to the value of its talented people, then the organization that does craft an effective Human

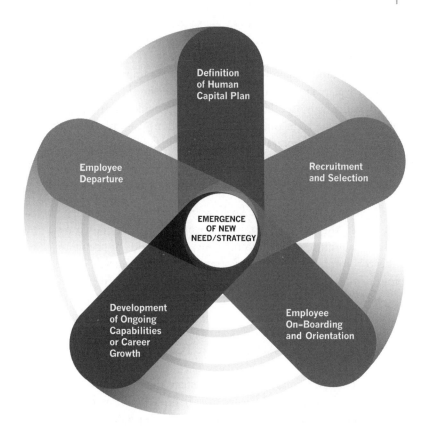

Capital plan stands to gain significant competitive advantage. The idea is simple: the organization that attracts and maintains more knowledgeable and talented performers than the competition tends to win market share.

Performers who possess the appropriate critical knowledge and talent are the ones who have the central body of knowledge, skill, experience, and wisdom necessary to drive a significant share of an organization's business performance. These people aren't mere space-fillers, mere successors to the highly talented employees who might be departing. These are the people who are often considered the "A-Level" players, the ones who consistently demonstrate superior performance and deliver exceptional results. Not only do they possess deep working knowledge about markets, customer needs, company processes, products and services, and innovative problem solving, but also they are the people who consistently know *how to get work done* effectively and efficiently.

These A-Level players also tend to improve an organization's profitability. Significantly. But they don't simply stop at improvement in profit margins.

A-Levels also constitute a significant share of the value of intangible assets and market capitalization. In short, these performers are critically important to *any* organization.

Many organizations operate under the false assumption that they have a solid workforce plan. Further, they presume that if they lack the proper number of talented individuals, the labor market will provide the right people with the right skills at the right time. These assumptions can unfortunately lead to disaster (as noted in Chapter 1, statistics suggest that the potential for such a disaster is likely to magnify in the coming years as the most talented employees become more and more scarce).

With all of this in mind, we turn our focus to the definition phase of the Human Capital Cycle. This stage lays the groundwork for avoiding shortfalls and disasters in the market for talented people. It insists upon a much more precise set of definitions for the competencies and kinds of people required to drive the core of an organization's strategic business model. The goal is to pinpoint the most qualified employees and prospects and then craft an effective plan around attracting and keeping those people.

GOALS AND OUTCOMES

Defining the Human Capital Plan is not a stage that should be taken lightly. Without it, the Human Capital Cycle will lack direction. It will fail to generate results at its highest efficiency. The organization that ignores or ineffectively undertakes this phase could lose out on that substantially higher profit potential, dramatically improved Human Resources efficiency, and significant advantage over the competition.

It is no understatement to suggest that each of the goals and outcomes listed in this section is of critical importance. Each tends to have a direct material effect on the welfare of an organization, its customers, and its employees.

All members of senior management should plan to review and foster these goals and outcomes as thoroughly as possible. Also, the Human Resources team should expect to play a central role in the process, as theirs is the paramount responsibility of translating the defined business strategy into a specific Human Capital Plan and its accompanying action steps.

DETERMINE HUMAN CAPITAL NEEDS

This first desired outcome is exactly why the HR team should be involved in any effort to define the Human Capital Plan. It is fine for an organization to determine its Human Capital needs, but if the people responsible for translating those needs into specific actions are not present (and contributing to the discussion), then this outcome becomes rather hollow.

In order to meet this outcome, senior management, in conjunction with the HR team, should plan to turn the search inward. This calls for researching and evaluating the organization's employees as thoroughly and as fairly as possible. Without a full understanding of where the organization currently stands, the management team cannot expect to accurately determine its current and future Human Capital needs.

ACCURATELY ASSESS CURRENT ORGANIZATIONAL CAPABILITIES

Senior management should also plan to conduct a thorough assessment of the organization's performance capacity. This means determining where the organization stands in the marketplace and how its employees contribute to success on an organizational and customer level. Knowing these current organizational capacities allows the senior management team to determine how far to raise the bar on future performance.

This outcome also provides the opportunity for senior management to examine how its current talent management, bench strength, and succession planning processes measure up to the ideal Human Capital Plan. The goal is to reach a thorough understanding of the gaps between present Human Capital capability and perceived Human Capital needs.

RECONCILE EXISTING TALENT MANAGEMENT, BENCH STRENGTH, AND SUCCESSION PLANNING PROCESSES

Once the senior management team has determined the gaps between present Human Capital capability and perceived Human Capital needs, the next logical step is to work with the HR department to develop ways to bridge those gaps.

DETERMINE THE MOST APPROPRIATE COMMUNICATION STRATEGY

Before moving forward on the implementation of the Human Capital Plan, senior management should plan to establish a system designed to search for both the intended and unintended consequences of said plan. Because this system should provide a fuller understanding of an organization's desired outcomes (and the capability to deliver on them) as well as undesirable outcomes, communication is certainly the most important element of the Human Capital Cycle, moving forward. Without proper communication, the system simply will not run at its maximum potential.

Perhaps the best choice for a comprehensive communication strategy is the double-loop feedback stream, as referenced in Chapter 3.

CLEARLY COMMUNICATE THE SITUATION, INTENTIONS, AND PLAN

This is arguably the most important outcome of defining the Human Capital Plan. While it is important to determine where the organization currently stands, where it needs to go on a Human Capital level, and how it hopes to get it there, it is perhaps more important to *communicate* that plan as clearly and thoroughly as possible. Everyone in the organization must understand the situation, intentions, and strategies to be implemented—everyone from senior management on down to the entry-level employee.

WHAT'S GOOD FOR THE ARMY . . .

The title of this section might give away the answer to this question, but on the global stage, where might you expect efficiency and talent to be of life and death importance? You guessed it: in the Army. Let's take a look at what one organization within the U.S. military has done to define its own Human Capital Plan.

The principal goal of this organization was to provide U.S. soldiers with the highest quality equipment at the right time and in the most cost-efficient manner. And according to General Peter J. Schoomaker, then the U.S. Army Chief of Staff, this was (and is) an incredibly important goal to fulfill (and to fulfill efficiently):

> Both the global war on terrorism and Army Transformation demand that our individual and organizational approach to our duties and tasks must reflect the seriousness and sense of urgency characteristic of an Army at war.

Considering the gravity of the situation, the question in General Shoomaker's mind was what, exactly, would the Army need to do in order to improve its organizational approach (and infuse it with the "sense of urgency" that he demanded)?

In answer to the question, this military organization established that it was time to implement what it called a "cultural transformation strategy." The strategy, they determined, would include the following four objectives:

1   Directly link strategic goals and objectives (leading to better consistency of purpose on all levels)
2   Improve and refine the focus of leadership, management, and technology on critical systems and processes
3   Influence new ways to manage, make fact-based decisions, and change the internal culture
4   Align metrics and reward systems with the strategic intent.

With objectives in hand, this military organization could take action from a top-down standpoint. Command-level decisions were made. It was determined that the best course of action would be to undertake what is called an Enterprise Excellence Federation (a holistic approach that boasts tools and techniques intended to achieve four specific objectives, each of which directly supported the objectives of the cultural transformation strategy outlined above). The Enterprise Excellence Federation objectives adopted by the Army were as follows:

• Improve and focus leadership, management, and technology on critical systems and processes
• Infuse a sense of urgency
• Establish a new way to manage, make fact-based decisions, and change the internal culture
• Focus first on the people.

The key enabler for the cultural transformation strategy was the focus on the people. With this new focus, the organization knew that it would find itself and its workforce in better position to adapt to change—and here we see the urgency demanded by Schoomaker. This enabler also allowed for a greater ability on the part of management to cope with the stress and demands of the duty.

From this people-first viewpoint, it was easy to see that an assessment of leadership was in order. To that end, six specific leadership competencies were identified:

- Leadership
- Teaming
- Communications
- Employee support
- Strategic thinking
- Fostering a positive organizational climate.

With all of this in place, this military organization could turn to determining and applying all the tools and techniques necessary to running an Enterprise Excellence Federation. As they discovered, these tools and techniques included a Quality Management System (QMS), a combination of Lean 6s and Six Sigma initiatives, the Capability Maturity Model Integrated (CMMI), the Voice of the Customer (VoC), and a leadership competencies development program.

General Shoomaker has since retired, but since the inception of the leadership competencies program, this military organization has conducted annual workforce surveys at nearly thirty locations to determine measurable progress in the routine use and observation of thirty specific behaviors (derived from the six specific leadership competencies listed above). In short, when it comes to meeting the leadership competencies, score improvements have ranged from 15 percent to 61 percent per site.

Today, feedback from people at the command-level confirms that the focus on these leadership competencies, thus far, has been the most significant contributor to the advancement of the necessary cultural transformation. According to many, it is the very reason that this military organization can expect to sustain lasting results.[2]

HOW TO BUILD THE DEFINITION OF THE HUMAN CAPITAL PLAN

We now turn to the specific steps that senior management should take in order to bring to fruition the general outcomes listed above. Each step in this seven-step process is of equal importance. They are aligned and cascaded through the four most typical organizational levels: the executive team, middle management, supervisory leaders, and individual contributors.

STEP 1: DEFINE THE OVERARCHING SUPPORT
TO THE NEW STRATEGY

It would be prudent for the management team to ask many questions of the organization's chief human capital officer (or equivalent). They should consider the following questions (and work with the HR representative to answer each of them before moving on to Step 2):

- How will our organization be affected by retirements?
- How are we actively preparing successors?
- Is the labor market currently prepared to replace or supplement our critical skills (in other words, are there enough A-Level people out there who are capable of replacing or supplementing our most talented performers)?
- How much employee turnover are we seeing in our most mission critical areas?
- What is this turnover costing the organization?
- What is it costing our customers?
- How are we currently addressing this turnover issue?
- Are we currently doing anything to create greater understanding of the financial consequences of our talent decisions?

The information that you uncover in asking and answering these questions will prove integral to the preparation of the Human Capital Plan.

STEP 2: DEFINE THE COMPETENCIES REQUIRED FOR SUPERIOR
PERFORMANCE IN THE NEW STRATEGY

With all of the information from Step 1 clearly established, senior management may now determine the most important components to moving the strategy forward. Step 2, in summary, is all about evaluating the best kinds of people available to fill the organization's Human Capital needs.

To that end, senior management should convene to discuss the following questions:

- What critical skills do we need in order to remain successful in the near to mid-term?
- What happens if we are unsuccessful in creating or acquiring those skills?
- What roles in our workforce provide the best value to our customers and generate the greatest return on our investment?

Talent is a significant driving force behind an organization's profitability and customer satisfaction. It is the central key to the Triple Win scenario. For this reason, the plan benefits greatly from the simple matter of assessing the organization's critical talent needs. The act of determining the most appropriate skills, knowledge, abilities, and motivations for each position within the organization can go a long way.

STEP 3: CONDUCT A CENSUS OR INVENTORY OF EMPLOYEE CAPABILITIES

Next, senior management should plan to assess the capabilities, competencies, and resources of the organization's current employee base (in order to see how it matches up with the ideal).

The best way to manage this step is to assess the critical talent levels of each current employee. For this assessment, we recommend considering ten specific leadership competencies:[3]

1. Decision making skills
2. Degree to which current performance exceeds expectations
3. Drive for results
4. Analytical skills
5. Potential to be successful in another function or department
6. Problem identification and resolution skills
7. Cognitive ability
8. Desire to develop others
9. Emotional maturity
10. Possession of global perspective.

To assess these competencies, current employee evaluation methods work quite well. Senior management might also decide to conduct a survey.

STEP 4: IDENTIFY SPECIFIC GAPS IN COMPETENCIES REQUIRED FOR SUCCESS

The senior management team should now have a complete understanding of where the organization stands in regards to its Human Capital and critical talent needs. The team has also conducted a census designed to assess the ten competencies of the current employee base. With these facts in hand, the team may now work to determine where the gaps between expected critical talent and actual critical talent are greatest. Every effort should be taken to ensure that the resulting report is as detailed and accurate as possible.

STEP 5: SET A COMPREHENSIVE, FAIR, AND EQUITABLE PROCESS TO ALIGN THE CURRENT RESOURCES—OR SECURE ADDITIONAL HUMAN CAPITAL

Once aware of the company gaps, the senior management team may now turn to outlining the most appropriate process to ensuring the highest quality of Human Capital. See Chapter 6 for more detail on the recruitment and selection of new employees.

STEP 6: VERIFY THE ALIGNMENT OF PROCESSES, SYSTEMS, POLICIES, PRACTICES, AND CULTURE

Of course a Human Capital Plan is effective only if it works in tandem with existing company policy. One cannot hope to engage in a plan that does not mesh with existing or future employees, their workflows, company policies and practices, or organizational culture.

Ensuring harmony between plan and culture requires the creation of an Employee Value Proposition that works in conjunction with the Human Capital Plan. If an Employee Value Proposition already exists within your organization, be sure to align the definition of your Human Capital Plan with that pre-existing proposition.

As noted previously, the Employee Value Proposition is a relatively new concept. It is clear, however, that its creation and application can be an important tool to underscore intended organizational culture. At the very least, it is an excellent way to reinforce a positive organizational climate in the event of change.

STEP 7: SET A COMMUNICATIONS STRATEGY

Again, communication is critical to any business strategy. The final step for the senior management team is to determine how it will gather feedback and evaluate the eventual performance of the Human Capital Plan. The team will need this information in order to make adjustments to the process, should adjustments be necessary.

Again, research suggests that the most efficient and effective communications strategy is known as the double-loop feedback stream (see Chapter 3).

The double-loop feedback stream is often where the subtleties and necessary refinements to the plan reveal themselves. Without the adjustments to the plan to which it leads, the likelihood of the organization achieving its targeted results declines dramatically.

THE HUMAN CAPITAL PLAN AT WORK

In the early 2000s, during a period of particularly explosive growth, Diane Limon of Sky International was looking to simplify and streamline the process of communication within her company. To that end, she decided that it was time to incorporate three of Sky's largest business units (all three being geographically centric but organizationally separate prior to the merger).

At the time, Limon had already come into her keen appreciation for the importance of Human Capital Management. So through her influence, there was created a clear understanding on the part of all members of the executive team that the newly merged organization's future market and financial success would be highly dependent upon its ability to quickly create an effective new culture. The intent was to define and pursue a nurturing culture that continuously scouted for talent and then diligently developed and applied that talent for the benefit of the organization, its customers, and its employees—the Triple Win.

Complicating the issue was the fact that Sky International, with its three largest units newly merged, found itself in the midst of a much more aggressive competitive environment. With the rise of several significant competitors at home and across the country, they now faced the immediate need to achieve substantial financial success. Not wanting to waste precious time, the members of the executive team quickly decided to take on the Human Capital Management initiatives themselves rather than doing what most executives do: pass the agenda to HR.

Limon, meanwhile, undertook a personal role in establishing a comprehensive approach to talent management. The ultimate goal was to create a culture that provided a common understanding of what constituted its critical knowledge and talent, identified where such talent resided, and then leveraged that knowledge and talent for the benefit of the organization and its customers.

The resultant Human Capital Plan included three distinct phases of work. The initial phase was an in-depth analysis to identify the critical knowledge and talent required to drive the desired performance of the business. Then, an organizational census (or inventory of knowledge and talent) was conducted. Finally, the census findings were applied to a full range of talent strategies, processes, systems, and measures to build a stronger bench of leadership and talented performers.

In the initial phase, considerable due diligence was applied to the goal of thoroughly understanding the reformed business model of the merged organization, its strategic objectives, cultural drivers, value proposition with its customers, and other dimensions of the operating systems. In-depth analyses produced a set of talent definitions that were unique to Sky International. Potential measures of business impact were also identified, and baseline data points were set for future comparative purposes. The work also uncovered special challenges and issues that needed to be addressed in order to accomplish the ultimate strategic targets.

One of the more challenging efforts for Limon and company was the creation of a talent census or inventory process. Great care was taken to establish a perception of fairness and equal opportunity across all levels of employees—as they were invited to self-declare their current skills and knowledge. Precisely orchestrated communications strategies were implemented with both leaders and associates to assure everyone of the sincere intent to discover, develop, and more strategically apply talent to achieve organizational goals.

The census findings provided a wealth of information for Sky's senior management team. Limon took it upon herself to ensure that the results were organized in a useful database for immediate and future data mining. Based upon these numbers, internal and external recruitment strategies were shaped to focus upon the needs and locations for critical knowledge and talent. New potential leaders were identified and moved into a variety of creative developmental paths.

Meanwhile, the development curriculum and processes were adjusted to center on critical knowledge and talent—and were expanded well beyond the typical classroom experiences. Curriculum now included project team assignments, career rotations, and new roles specifically structured to deliver learning opportunities; all of which in turn facilitated greater ease in sharing knowledge and experience.

Perhaps most importantly, Limon and the rest of the senior management team led the way in seeking opportunities to coach, mentor, and provide feedback to all critical talent performers. The performance management process was thus aligned and more rigorously practiced. The criteria for promotions, rewards, and other forms of performance recognition were then redesigned and aligned with the Human Capital Plan.

Within eighteen months of the determination to pursue this new Human Capital approach, Limon was able to report the realization of a more unified organizational culture—and better yet, far more positive financial results.

SUMMARY

Defining the Human Capital Plan sets the groundwork for strategic success. We reiterate the key steps that senior management from all functions (and especially the chief human capital officer) need to address:

1. Define the overarching support to the new strategy
2. Define the competencies (the skills, knowledge, abilities, and motivations) required for superior performance in the new strategy
3. Conduct a census or inventory of employee capabilities
4. Identify specific gaps in competencies required for success
5. Set a comprehensive, fair, and equitable process to align the current resources—or secure additional Human Capital
6. Verify the alignment of processes, systems, policies, practices, and culture
7. Set a communications strategy.

As demonstrated by Sky International, careful pursuit of these key tasks can produce beneficial results for your organization. Your customers, constituents, and employees will see positive results as well.

Chapter

6

RECRUITMENT AND SELECTION

Wᴵᵀʜ ᴛʜᴇ ᴅᴇꜰɪɴɪᴛɪᴏɴ of the Human Capital Plan in place, we turn our sights to the process of recruiting and selecting highly talented individuals. As was highlighted in Chapter 1, the pool of potential managers gets drier every year. In the near future, many companies stand to face a serious managerial crisis. The solution to this common predicament may seem obvious (the company in crisis must recruit more talented people than the competition), but a strategy is required beyond simply saying, "We need to recruit more talented people." The senior management team must implement a process not only to attract the most talented individuals in their field, but also to retain them, as well.

This chapter reveals a range of tips and strategies to help make this otherwise lofty goal a reality. Studies have shown that it is the organization that implements these tips and strategies that experiences the business success of the Triple Win. For many organizations, the recruitment and selection process outlined in the following pages may seem like a considerable undertaking. While it might have its difficulty in the early going, the beauty of the Human Capital Cycle is that it promotes ease of use in the long run. And make no mistake, significant rewards accompany the completion of this stage.

Recent history suggests that there have been times when the high-quality labor supply outstripped the demand. Shifts in the labor market are continuous and follow economic cycles. But a focus on effective recruitment remains paramount. Hiring a new manager might once have been little more than a matter of picking up the phone. There was also a time when recruiting people from other firms might have been a simple proposition. But data suggests many troubling trends that will likely stymie the effectiveness of traditional recruitment and selection strategies in coming years.

Myriad statistics demonstrate the sheer force of modern worker unrest. Shifts in the labor market will be further exacerbated by the restlessness of the 83 percent of current employees who are expected to be actively searching for new employment by 2009.[1] According to a survey conducted by *The Economist*, this is because at least a third of these people are reportedly being actively recruited by other potential employers.[2]

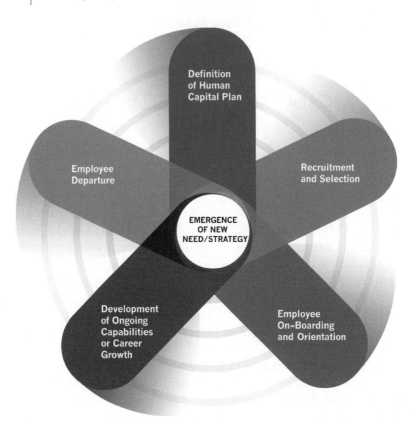

The time and money commitments associated with these trends are sure to be substantial. The same recruitment and selection processes are costing more and more each year. About 78 percent of respondents to *The Economist* survey report that it is taking *longer* to find talent. One study by the Corporate Executive Board (CEB) suggested at least a 38 percent increase in the average recruitment time period. For the most part, the average time to fill a position has been reported at 30 to 90 days.[3]

In addition to the time crunch, a money crunch has been observed, as well. In a Performance and Talent Management Trend Survey conducted by the Business Performance Management Forum and released in March, 2007, 95 percent of respondents reported that the cost of acquiring talent rose in 2006. The cost increase averaged 20 percent to 25 percent. It has gotten so bad that companies in the United States are reportedly spending nearly 50 times as much to acquire a $100,000 salaried professional when compared to the development investments in the career of that same professional.

It is clear that the labor market is shrinking for a host of reasons. Chief among them: the shift in the experience level of the market; the changing criteria for critical knowledge and talent; the nature of the global talent pool; the competition for talent; the restlessness of existing employee populations; and rising costs and recruitment timelines. All of these factors should be sufficient to spark renewed attention to the effectiveness and efficiency of current recruitment strategies.

GOALS AND OUTCOMES

Considering the complex and intertwined nature of the trend factors facing the current and near-term labor markets, the desired outcomes of this stage of the Human Capital Cycle seem to rise in importance. The Triple Win is simply not possible for the company that does not find success in the following outcomes.

PROMPTLY IDENTIFY THE RIGHT PEOPLE WITH THE RIGHT SKILLS FOR OPEN OR SOON-TO-BE OPEN POSITIONS

The entire recruitment and selection stage cannot operate (at least not properly) until the organization identifies exactly who it wants to recruit and select for open positions. Of the three outcomes outlined here, this one should be considered the most urgent—at the very least, the senior management team should plan on determining the right people with the right skills in a reasonable timeframe.

Assuming that senior management has already achieved the goals and outcomes of the definition stage of the Human Capital Cycle, it should already know what types of people the organization will need in order to formulate the Triple Win. This outcome calls for the senior management to apply that knowledge in an active search for the ideal recruits. In other words, the team begins by determining and defining the organization's Human Capital needs. Then, it looks to the pool of available candidates to select all those who best fill those needs.

CREATE AN EMPLOYEE VALUE PROPOSITION AND BRANDING

For most organizations in need of more qualified recruits, the Employee Value Proposition (EVP) is too often passed over. This is a shame because this outcome is perhaps the most important when it comes to recruiting and retaining key employees.

The EVP for an organization can be understood as a reflection of the employment experience that individuals have while a member of that organization. It refers to the complete package of experiences and benefits employees are likely to gain in return for their contribution, effort, creativity, commitment and loyalty. Importantly it establishes, formally or informally, an implicit agreement or "psychological contract" between an individual and an organization, between employee and employer.

Employment branding refers to how the work experience for an employee for a particular organization is portrayed to current and prospective employees. It is important to align the employment brand with the EVP, and to develop an EVP prior to developing an employment brand. If the brand that is portrayed to current and prospective employees is not in line with the actual work experience expressed in the Employee Value Proposition, there is a risk of losing employees who become disillusioned.[4]

In order to understand an organization's unique Employee Value Proposition, the organization should engage employees in qualitative discussions about their work experience, and organize focus groups with employees to identify gaps between the actual and the ideal, with a view to fill those gaps.

It is important to engage A-Level performers in discussions about work experience in order to craft a compelling EVP. The employees included should look like and act as much like the prospective employees an organization would like to hire as possible. To do this, organizations must first identify the kind of current employees that are most critical to their future competitiveness and growth as these are kinds of people the organization aspires to bring on board. It is also important for organizations to consider why potential leaders would want to work for them.

Focus groups, interviews, informal conversations and town hall meetings are likely to yield rich and meaningful information which can be used to create a winning EVP. Organizations should strive to express the EVP in terms of what members of the organization do as opposed to what they say.

Key categories of employee values can be summarized as follows:

- Organizational-specific attributes (corporate appeal, working conditions, social responsibility, culture, work–life balance, social activities)
- Leadership-specific attributes (management style, feedback, recognition, reward)
- Work design and career-specific attributes (opportunities for promotion, advancement, training, exciting and challenging work)
- Financial-specific attributes (direct and indirect financial rewards, salary, pay rate, benefits).

While financial compensation will likely be among the topics discussed in conversations with employees, it is usually not the most important value expressed by employees. Employee values are deeper than "pay" and "benefits" and are more likely linked to aspects such as pride associated with working for a particular company, the organization's corporate conduct and ethics; respect that individuals receive from other associates within the organization, work–life balance issues and opportunities for advancement.[5]

CONSIDER STRATEGIES TO REDUCE THE COST OF PLACEMENT

It is fine to select the right people and then create the perfect message to send to those people, but unless the senior management team considers ways to keep low the cost of recruiting and orienting those people, the entire effort might wind up failing. So the final outcome of the recruitment and selection stage must be to consider and implement a carefully organized, systemic recruitment and selection process that qualifies candidates in ways that reduces the cost outlay overall.

Keeping costs low is paramount, but the senior management team should avoid going overboard with its cost-cutting efforts. For some highly qualified individuals, the experience of a low-budget recruiting process might be a deal-breaker. So the most successful companies seek a balance. For the median prospects, the cost outlay must remain low. The company should then reserve the more expensive recruiting techniques for the most highly qualified prospects.

The above might seem like an overly simplified list of desired outcomes, but it all points to one overarching outcome: *Develop a fair, efficient, and effective recruitment and selection process.* The outcomes list sets up the essential target of having a legally sound recruitment and selection process that also produces the perception of fairness. And in the end, the company that reaches all of these desired outcomes will be left with a high-powered, highly effective, and low-cost recruiting strategy.

PROCESSING A STRATEGY

George Hermans was the general manager of a food processing plant called Universal Food Processing (UFP). UFP was in need of recruitment and selection at nearly all positions in the plant—everything from leadership on down to front-line processor roles—so Hermans knew that his experience in the subject would prove a valuable asset.

Hermans' first course of action was to determine exactly who he needed in order to fill the many vacancies coming due at the plant. Given that UFP was a food processing plant—and that quality standards in that particular industry are extremely high—Hermans had to pay close attention to how those standards would apply to all aspects of the business. So he launched a detailed investigation to define the full set of critical knowledge, skills, abilities, and motivations that would be required for people in the various leader and front-line roles at the plant. The work design, process flow, quality process requirements, and distribution of day-to-day operational duties were simultaneously identified.

When the points of integration and subtle nuances of competency definitions were complete, the recruitment and selection process could then be constructed. While UFP did not establish an Employee Value Proposition *per se*, the recruitment strategy did incorporate a marketing approach (or branding of the anticipated work environment) in order to attract the desired set of initial candidates. The effort was to make UFP seem attractive to exactly the kinds of people Hermans felt were needed: highly talented individuals who not only wanted to work in an entirely unique cultural environment but also were willing and eager to accept greater than normal responsibility for the company's stringent quality and production standards.

These two clear messages were projected at every opportunity within the labor market. Hermans felt that if his company could do this—and that it led to the recruitment of exactly the kind of individuals he was looking for—then UFP would enjoy an environment of higher than average employee empowerment, a relatively flat, team-centric organizational structure, and a culture of high-quality performance.

Now, fortunately for Hermans, this particular sector boasted a full cupboard when it came to potential candidates. In fact, UFP ran into a different kind of problem: they received thousands of candidates for their open positions.

In order to handle all this incoming traffic, the recruitment process was established as a pipeline or funnel designed to more inexpensively process the thousands of initial candidates. Simpler, less expensive techniques and tools were used to quickly and accurately qualify each individual among the masses. As the pipeline or funnel progressed and a smaller pool of pre-qualified candidates could be identified, more complex and somewhat more expensive techniques were used. These included behavioral assessment simulations, behavioral interviewing techniques, panel interviews, and other unique motor skill assessments. All of the techniques were then carefully matched to the precise list of critical skills, knowledge, abilities, and motivations established by Hermans.

Perhaps most importantly, anyone who participated in any capacity within the recruitment and selection process received intensive training in the accurate application of all techniques and tools. Each person who played an active role in the recruitment and selection process was expected to thoroughly understand the rigor of the process as well as the intended strategic targets.

Since the physical facility housing the plant was actually in the act of being built, the timing of the employee recruitment and selection process would have to coincide with the completion of the plant. This way, upon completion of the selection process, the new employees would be able to promptly come into the new facility and commence their extensive orientation.

After the process was launched, Hermans and UFP continued to do their homework. In the weeks to come, the efficiency and effectiveness of the recruitment and selection process was consistently and closely monitored. Intentionally designed double-loop feedback was incorporated to quickly make any adjustments. And finally, highly detailed and accurate candidate tracking systems were used to document all steps (as well as the corresponding results for each candidate).

The results of the start-up operation proved better than anticipated. It was with great pride that George Hermans and the new organization were able to report meeting production and quality standards within a fraction of the previous operational timeframes of the parent company. The facility became a showcase of not only its physical plant, but more importantly, the way in which an organization should be assembled and operated. Incidentally (but not coincidentally), the measurable results also exceeded the expectations for return on invested capital.

The moral of the story? The act of branding the work experience directly led UFP to a highly successful recruitment and selection process. More than that, however, it contributed to the effectiveness and satisfaction of all the candidates recruited. The intent was to presage the employment experience with the quality and nature of the recruitment process—and this wound up paying dividends for the company on a revenue as well as efficiency level.

HOW TO RECRUIT AND SELECT CRITICAL TALENT

With the goals and outcomes aligned, we may turn to the task of outlining exactly *how* to implement the recruitment and selection stage. The first step in any process is to determine the desired outcome. Thanks to the definition stage, the organization should already be well aware of its vacancies and impending vacancies. The next step, then, is to determine exactly *who* is available to fill those vacancies and how to recruit them. The specific key tasks that follow are designed to do exactly that.

STEP 1: IDENTIFY A TALENT MARKET WITH A HIGH LEVEL OF PRIME CANDIDATES

With the company's needs defined and the prime candidates determined, the first step in the recruitment process is to determine exactly *where* those prime candidates can be found. Many organizations may decide that the local talent pool is rich enough to fulfill its needs. Others may realize that a more national (or even global) search is required.

The senior management team must determine the specific pool from which to draw. The pool might include seasoned and talented executives from competing firms; it might include all those factory workers in the region with five or more years of experience; it might include employees in other positions within the organization itself; it might include entry-level recruits from specific universities; and everything in between.

Once the team has reached an understanding of where it needs to turn to fill a given position or positions, it may move on to crafting a message to send to that very specific pool of recruits.

STEP 2: ALIGN ALL ACTIONS WITH THE EMPLOYEE VALUE PROPOSITION

The definition and significance of the Employee Value Proposition has already been covered in great detail, but what of its applicability? It is important to remember that an EVP is something that is used to target specific individuals. It is like an advertisement to all of those people targeted for all of those roles needed to be filled. Since that is the case, it would be ridiculous to think that the EVP is a static entity. Recruiting different types of people (and for different roles) requires differing messages. One cannot recruit for sales in the same way that one recruits for the accounting department. Specifically dedicated messages must be crafted for each discipline.

The senior management team should not plan to advertise the organization as some kind of chameleon—one that bends and alters its culture in order to adhere to the ideal for *every* type of employee out there. Instead, it should adhere to the measures of branding. The brand defines the corporate culture. The EVP projects that culture to a specific pool of recruits in a tailored and dedicated way.

The EVP(s) created should align with the types of recruits desired. To this end, the following questions should be answered:

- What does the ideal recruit have to gain by working for this organization?
- What aspects of this company will appeal to these recruits?
- How does our corporate culture align with the career philosophy of these recruits?

The best way to determine what a prospective employee can hope to gain from joining an organization is to interview the people currently holding those positions. It is one thing to assume an organization's key points of attractiveness and entirely another to actually investigate them. Getting the details from the ground floor—or at least from the wing of the organization that requires more recruits—is the best and most accurate way to tailor an EVP to a specific recruiting need.

If an overarching survey of the organization's employees is out of the question, then it might be prudent to undertake a more direct approach to gathering data: set up focus groups. Whether these focus groups are assembled and conducted by someone outside the organization or within the existing HR department does not matter. What does matter is that, first, everyone from the senior management team in position to make recruiting decisions attends the focus group meetings, and second, all employees in attendance are aware that they may make honest and direct comments without the fear of being reprimanded. With these two conditions met, the senior management team can proceed with confidence that it has gathered accurate and meaningful recruiting information. That information may then be formulated into a dedicated EVP.

STEP 3: PREPARE THE REMAINING DETAILS OF THE RECRUITMENT AND SELECTION PLAN

With candidate needs determined, the pool from which to draw candidates identified, and the Employee Value Proposition defined, the team may move on to preparing the remaining details of the recruitment and selection plan. These details are very specific and equally critical to the success of the program.

The senior management team must implement systems, policies, and practices that align appropriately with the desired process. Without such alignment, the organization cannot be certain that it will experience an efficient pipeline of qualified candidates. Nor can it be certain that it is providing equal opportunities to the qualified candidates to begin with. Highly talented candidates could be lost to the inefficiency of the system.

The best way for the team to do this is to create materials and objectives that thoroughly prepare all interviewers and decision makers for this new standard of recruiting and selecting employees. Such rigorous preparation will surely make for a consistent, fair, cost-effective, and high-quality process.

STEP 4: CREATE A CANDIDATE TRACKING PROCESS

Many companies are successful at implementing a high-quality recruitment and selection process. Too many companies then fail in the follow-up. No system is perfect. And even if the company experiences a large influx of candidates during Week 1, that does not mean that they are necessarily the *perfect* candidates. Nor does it mean that the recruiters will successfully bring in the highest quality individuals.

The only way to guarantee a successful recruitment and selection effort is to document all key steps and findings in a candidate tracking process. As many details as possible should be catalogued—everything from the number of recruits who applied to specific recruits' educational and career background to the level of success enjoyed by each recruiter.

This information must then be passed back to the decision makers on the senior management team. The best and most efficient way to turn that information into action (and exact adjustments to the process, as needed) is through a secure double-loop feedback stream.

RECRUITMENT AND SELECTION AT WORK

Sky International's roots had been with designing buildings for the mid-sized corporate market. Then, as they grew, Sky began working with larger customers with more than 10,000 employees. But about four years ago, Limon's call for in-depth market research led to a very intriguing discovery. The report illustrated a relatively high majority of customer dissatisfaction within the market Sky had so recently vacated. Realizing that they stood to seize a competitive share of a multibillion dollar market, Limon and the rest of management determined that the best course of action would be to launch an aggressive re-entry into the highly competitive middle market while attempting to maintain their position with the larger accounts.

In the midst of the senior managers' discussion of the business strategy, they realized that their greatest challenge would be in the Human Capital arena. A new sales culture (capable of delivering superior performance) would be needed if their sales team was going to realize the full potential of the market opportunity. In short, that culture would never come to fruition unless Sky brought more quality salespeople on board.

Another element to consider was the timing. Limon had been around long enough to know that you can't snap up market share—even in the relatively slow-moving world of architectural design—without keeping the operational tempo urgent. So she knew that the company needed to be capable of producing high business volume at a fast pace. Ultimately, Sky made the decision to recruit and develop an entirely new sales force that could focus all of its energies on the market of re-entry.

While the sales strategy was being refined, the Human Capital Plan was set into urgent motion. Simultaneously (and in collaboration), both the recruitment and selection process as well as a comprehensive development process were tailored to fit the business and cultural needs of the organization.

The company then set out to define the critical role requirements for the position of sales representative. All those operating within this new market would have to fit these requirements perfectly. Great professional care was deployed in gathering the foundational information, analyzing the data, and verifying the accuracy of twelve sales competencies and personal characteristics that were unique to this new position and culture. This set of competencies and characteristics was called a "success profile." It included detailed competency labels and supportive behavioral definitions.

One interesting point reached by the success profile was that it would benefit Sky to avoid recruiting seasoned architectural sales representatives. This was because Limon and the HR team believed that such candidates would arrive with a set of habits and pre-established opinions about how to conduct sales activities. And it seemed foolish to ask new employees to unlearn old techniques.

Once defined, Sky put the entire strategy on a fast track. The front-end work to identify competencies, create the success profile, set up the recruitment strategy steps, establish the branding and appeal in the talent marketplace, and prepare the recruitment and selection process occurred in a matter of weeks.

Given the urgency of the matter, Limon knew that additional help would be needed. So the members of the recruitment team included more than just representatives from Sky's HR department. They also brought in a few professionals from outside the company—a recruiting agency that had a track record of success in sales recruiting as well as rapid hiring. Between Sky and this recruiting agency, a high-powered recruitment strategy was formed—one that would target specific geographies, campuses, and branding to quickly attract qualified candidates.

Sky provided a companion selection guide and training to all recruiting agency and employer representatives who were involved in the recruitment and selection process. In the guide, the recruiter would find detailed job requirements, sample application descriptions of the competency in action, behavioral evidence that constitutes a good match, behavioral interview questions, and guidelines for evaluating the candidate. The interviewers were asked to rate each candidate based on their degree of proficiency or demonstrated presence of each competency and characteristic listed in the guide. This scoring would prove to be critical, as it didn't just aid in the process of selecting candidates, but in successfully (and quickly) orienting them to the company, as well.

For Sky International, the planning might have been excellent, but the recruitment process still proved intense. The HR team (in tandem with the external recruiting agency) tracked the progress of candidates on a daily basis. Once the targeted number of sales recruits was reached, Sky sent out its offers. For the most part, those offers were accepted within one to two weeks. And by the end of the following week, the newly hired sales representatives had reported for the orientation and development process.

It is important to note that the combined strategy for recruitment, selection, orientation, and development undertaken by Sky worked (and worked quite well). Early anecdotal and leading indicator evidence began to emerge within just weeks after the completion of the development cycle. The first sale for Limon's new sales force was reported within three weeks (and this was from within a business environment that often takes six months or more to create). Several weeks later, one of the sales representatives had already earned a ranking as a top performer.[6]

SUMMARY

As Sky International demonstrates, exploration and careful pursuit of the key steps produces a Triple Win—for the organization, its customers, and the employees. In summary, the key steps include the following:

1. Identify a talent market with a high level of prime candidates
2. Align all actions with the Employee Value Proposition
3. Prepare the remaining details of the recruitment and selection plan
4. Create a candidate tracking process.

7

EMPLOYEE ON-BOARDING
AND ORIENTATION

W HILE EMPLOYEE orientation might seem like a natural progression from the recruitment and selection stage, it is certainly a more difficult process to quantify. Compared with other Human Capital Management practices, employee on-boarding or orientation has been the subject of relatively few studies. The studies we do have to draw from, however, seem to suggest that this particular stage of the Human Capital Cycle is nearly impossible to ignore.

Drawing from available data, the Andersen Human Capital Group has determined that organizations that deploy human resource practices such as new hire orientation or on-boarding (including performance expectations) and then regularly discharge low performers tend to achieve greater total shareholder return (TSR) over a period averaging three to five years. Other studies show that 15–30 percent of the total market value of an organization may be attributed to Human Capital Management practices. With this study, however, no specific percentage was ascribed to employee on-boarding or orientation.[1]

Organizations that adhere to this stage of the Human Capital Cycle also tend to enjoy smoother operations. Those companies that exceed the expected on-boarding processes are more likely to reduce the employee turnover caused by a lack of growth and development opportunities. In other words, they are far less likely to view employee retention as a widespread problem.[2]

Studies suggest that organizational leaders have only a four to six month window in which to successfully integrate newly hired employees into their new environment.[3] Traditional approaches to on-boarding have been conducted in a relatively *ad hoc* manner. For the most part, this means inconsistency and lack of discipline in the process. In fact, the disorganized manner itself has contributed heavily to the 40–50 percent of new senior-level associates who fail to perform or achieve their targeted results.[4]

What these few studies suggest is that a more comprehensive and high-powered process is needed. The Human Capital Cycle represents that process.

This stage has the benefit of quickly activating the critical knowledge and talent of a newly hired employee. The on-boarding process that properly

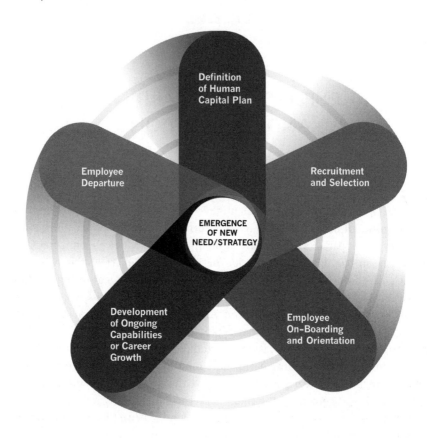

reflects the Employee Value Proposition helps alleviate (or even eliminate) the unsettling period of ennui, confusion, disappointment, and disillusionment experienced by most new employees. Put another way, a quick orientation process prevents new staff from experiencing buyer's remorse about joining the organization.

GOALS AND OUTCOMES

Given the nature of employee on-boarding and orientation—that it contributes to a significant portion of organizational success, requires a speedy delivery, and directly influences the first impressions of most highly talented new employees—it is fair to say that it is extremely important to achieve the outcomes that follow. Depending on how it is conducted, this stage of the Human Capital Cycle has the potential to do one of two things: either it sets talented people on the performance fast track or it sends them fleeing for another offer. The organization that adheres to the following outcomes will find Triple Win success.

INITIATE NEW EMPLOYEES INTO THEIR ASSIGNED ROLES EFFECTIVELY AND EFFICIENTLY

This is the first outcome for good reason: it is paramount and most certainly central to the process. Regardless how much preparation the senior management team makes, regardless how rigorous the structure of the process implemented, if it does not produce results in the area of motivated, knowledgeable, and highly talented individuals, then it has failed.

Due to the nature of employee turnover and the Human Capital Cycle, the more efficient the on-boarding process, the better. This is because the quicker a new hire moves from Day One of orientation to Day One on the job, the more likely he/she is to stick around for any appreciable amount of time.

CLARIFY PERFORMANCE EXPECTATIONS—ESPECIALLY ON THE APPLICATION OF CRITICAL KNOWLEDGE AND TALENT

It is possible to train a new employee efficiently and effectively, but then fail to demonstrate to him/her what he/she is expected to do on a daily basis. A sales team, for example, might learn all the ins and outs of the marketplace and the preferred methodology to sell, but if they do not know their performance milestones, they have nothing to shoot for. This tends to lead to complacency, which obviously leads to a lack of optimal production.

The same goes for on-boarding and orientation. The more a new hire knows about what is expected of him/her during the orientation process, the more likely he/she will be to see it through to the end (and perform up to expectations during the interim). If they are made privy to the evaluation methodology that their new employers intend to use, then they will be more willing and capable participants in the process.

Some performance expectations for the senior management team to consider: propensity to meet targeted business results, grasp of the Employee and Customer Value Proposition, understanding of the business cycle and economic landscape of the field in which they have been hired, and a mastery of all subject matter imparted during the on-boarding process.

HEIGHTEN EMPLOYEE ENGAGEMENT IN THE PROCESS

It is one thing to dictate to a group of new hires. It is entirely another to allow them to become willing participants. The more the new hires are engaged in orientation, the more effective the program will be. This is because hands-on work in which an employee may take part has the benefit of validating that employee's decision on choosing a given company as his/her employer. If they feel empowered, they will appreciate their career decision all the more.

The organization that considers breaking up classroom sessions with sessions in the field often completes this outcome efficiently. Class work should be injected with more lively opportunities to spend a week or two in the field or even take the occasional field trip to various units of the organization (such as a customer service center) to see firsthand how business is conducted.

DELIVER TO THE NEW HIRES A CLEAR UNDERSTANDING OF THE HUMAN CAPITAL CYCLE

The employee who cannot see where he/she is heading is not likely to stay with the organization. The organization that communicates the concepts that fuel the Human Capital Cycle will find success in the on-boarding and orientation stage. If new hires have the opportunity to see the various stages of the cycle, they will better understand what is expected of them, as well as what they might expect from their job. In the end, this leads to greater employee retention and far more efficient and effective orientation.

All four of these outcomes are critical. The company that completes them secures a quicker return on each new employee, and therefore improved business results.

PROCESSING NEW HIRES . . .

When Universal Food Processing (UFP) managers had completed their recruitment and selection process, they turned their sights toward implementing a series of well-planned orientation sessions for the new employee group. Given the nature of the industry—and the tight strictures on food quality—these sessions included rigorous technical training, equipment operation training, and careful instructions on how to adhere to the tightly regulated processing standards. Pretty standard for a manufacturing or processing environment.

What wasn't as standard was how George Hermans and the other members of the board conducted themselves during the orientation phase. These leaders directly engaged in hands-on, in-depth discussion about the plant's mission, its vision for greatness, its values (including how those values had guided their recruitment and selection process), and the day-to-day performance competencies expected of each employee. The reason they subscribed to this hands-on approach was simple: they knew that if they personally and thoroughly related UFP's mission, vision, and values, they would impart an indelible personal connection with each employee. Further, each new hire would better recognize their unique contribution to organizational performance. And Hermans knew that this would lead to greater employee engagement and accountability for results.

During orientation, Hermans and the other leaders focused on establishing the lean leadership hierarchy and the teamwork design structure. They outlined the expectation that all employees become especially skilled in collaborative teaming behaviors. Among those behaviors:

- The engagement in team governance
- The contribution to work direction
- The accountability for a variety of work and administrative responsibilities
- The measurement of quality and production standards
- The continual fostering of a productive, high-performance culture.

With these concepts and models in place—and through UFP's preference for action-oriented learning—the orientation team was able to quickly convert conceptual material into hands-on experience and new team skills.

The success of this orientation process (combined with the recruitment and selection stage of the Human Capital Cycle) proved much more significant than expected. In fact, a few of the more stringent quality and production throughput levels were reached within a mere three weeks of the start of the operation. Compare this to the previous benchmark of 36 *months* in other similar operations. Given this staggering dichotomy, it was easy for Hermans to see that he had gotten a healthy return on invested capital for his company. The relatively heavy amount of capital invested would be paid back in spades by the production of these highly motivated and well-trained new hires.

Naturally, the results of UFP's orientation process were a cause for celebration. But more than that, they served as a constant reminder of the level of business results that may be achieved by an organization with Human Capital foresight.

So what is the moral of the story? UFP's orientation process incorporated four factors that are particularly important to infusing meaning and purpose within an employee's work. This includes:

- Work that is motivating
- Work that cultivates a sense of belonging, community, and emotional bonding
- Work that instills pride in its core mission
- Work that has clear strategic direction and a direct line of sight for every individual who contributes to the organization's performance.[5]

HOW TO CONDUCT EMPLOYEE ORIENTATION

The desired outcomes of this stage of the Human Capital Cycle obviously go hand in hand with the desired outcomes of the recruitment and selection stage. Recruitment and selection is only as valuable as the high-quality employees it generates. Similarly, the on-boarding and orientation process is only as valuable as the high-quality employees it trains and retains. The specific steps that follow are designed with these points in mind.

STEP 1: LINK EACH EMPLOYEE ROLE TO ITS CORRESPONDING STRATEGIC OUTCOME

Before implementing the process, the senior management team should plan to document what is expected of each employee role involved in the hiring process. If the role is sales, then the team should map out the best strategic outcome for sales. For customer service, proper levels of customer satisfaction should be determined.

This step has a three-headed benefit. First, it clarifies and documents all outcomes for the senior management team. Second, it helps instil a sense of direction for the new hires. Third, it ensures that all customers will receive the highest quality support from those same new hires.

STEP 2: ESTABLISH SPECIFIC EXPECTATIONS FOR ROLES, RESPONSIBILITIES, AND STANDARDS OF PERFORMANCE

Certainly, there will be much expected of all new employees. In many cases, they will have big shoes to fill. In others, they will have entirely new roles to fill—ones that the company itself has never managed. In either case, if the new hire is not made aware of his/her roles, responsibility, and performance expectations, he/she will flounder in his/her new career environment.

The best way for the senior management team to ensure that this does not happen is to regularly measure the new hire's performance. But if this is to occur, the new hire also has to be made aware of the evaluation methodology that the team intends to employ. All testing or other performance measurements should include the employee's retention of the orientation material, capability to perform within his/her assigned role, and grasp of the unique features of the marketplace.

Most successful on-boarding processes include regular testing in order for the employee to reach the subsequent phase. The employee must be made aware of expectations on these tests if he/she is to perform well. If additional licensure is required for the new hire to operate within the marketplace, he/she needs to be made aware of those requirements, as well.

STEP 3: DEMONSTRATE THE EMPLOYEE VALUE PROPOSITION

The Employee Value Proposition is the lifeblood of any successful on-boarding process. It is the most direct line to the employee on why he/she might have chosen this particular organization for which to work. The clearer the EVP, the greater the validation of an employee's career decision.

For the recent college graduate, a clear EVP imparts the notion that he/she might want to consider a long career with the chosen organization. For those who were already thriving in the industry, the EVP invigorates and affirms their decision to join the organization. For those few who have come from elsewhere (or even those who have struggled in the field in the past), the EVP serves as a beacon of hope that this new career will be the answer.

STEP 4: EQUIP NEW EMPLOYEES WITH ESSENTIAL KNOWLEDGE ABOUT THE ORGANIZATION, ITS CUSTOMERS, AND ITS PARTNERS

The Triple Win is not possible unless each new employee knows the rigors of the three bodies involved. Unless all new hires are given a clear understanding of what it takes to find success within the organization, with its customers, and with its partners, they will not be able to perform to their highest potential—and neither will the organization.

STEP 5: CONNECT NEW HIRES TO PEOPLE FROM WHOM THEY CAN LEARN

The first (and often the most effective) technique to completing this step is to assign each new hire to a dedicated mentor. The mentor would ideally be someone with experience in the same role in which the new hire will be operating. He/she should be encouraged to train the new hire on daily operations, what to expect, and offer tips on how to perform at a high level. The mentor and new hire should be asked to complete actual working tasks together. This way, connections between coworkers are fostered in real problem solving environments.

The mentoring technique has two added benefits, as well. First, the learning process for the new hire tends to accelerate dramatically. Second, the mentor—through regular evaluations of the new hire's skills and progress—can communicate to the senior management team the level of critical knowledge and talent that the new hire brings to the organization.

These days, many companies have also turned to technology-driven social networks in order to connect new hires with each other as well as existing employees. Social networking tools like LinkedIn, Skype, and MySpace have proven to be particularly effective in fostering a community environment. And whether the community in question exists in virtual space or within pre-established communities of practice, the mentor should help adapt the new hire to the current culture.

One final (and often overlooked) technique is to station new hires in physical space that engenders natural opportunities for communication and collaboration with others. A remote or disconnected location presents special challenges that require extra effort in communications.

STEP 6: PROVIDE NETWORK MAPS OF PEOPLE

An employee that knows the lay of the land within the organization is far more efficient than one who does not. The first step toward learning that sort of thing is knowing who exactly works for the organization. In this way, one key resource for the new hire is a tool that he/she might use to find any given employee within the organization. This tool is known as a network map. It might be considered the yellow pages of the company.

One excellent tool that the executive team could use to create such a network map is known as the Social Network Analysis tool (SNA).

STEP 7: FACILITATE A LEARNING ENVIRONMENT IN WHICH EMPLOYEES CAN FEEL COMFORTABLE.

The comfortable classroom is the effective classroom. If a new hire is not comfortable in the environment in which he/she is expected to learn—and contributing factors to that environment range from the quality of the instructor to the comfort of the chairs to the lighting in the room—then he/she cannot be expected to learn at his/her highest capacity. To this end, new hires should be encouraged to astutely observe situations, listen carefully, and ask cogent questions.

It is also important not to smother the new hire in the on-boarding and orientation process. Sufficient private time for creativity and reflection is often beneficial. Studies at both Harvard and MIT have shown significant jumps in productivity when a new hire is offered private time without distractions. By contrast, learning productivity is deleteriously affected by frequent interruptions.

EMPLOYEE ORIENTATION AT WORK

With its recruiting and selecting program in place, Sky International was able to begin engaging its brain trust—along with outside consulting resources— to design and deliver an accelerated, comprehensive, and systemic approach to orienting its new sales staff. Limon knew that she would need to impart the sales skills and product knowledge related to the re-entry market as quickly and efficiently as possible. Otherwise, the company would stand to lose market share.

The systematic process of new hire orientation, on-boarding, business training, customer service training, and sales training represented a groundbreaking, significantly different approach to the rapid development of a new sales force in approximately 100 days. Given that the usual timeframe for an undertaking such as this stands at approximately six to eighteen months, Limon believed herself justified in feeling proud of the board's efforts.

But how did they manage to design, develop, and deliver a sales performance training and coaching system in such remarkable time?

Limon first assembled a project team made up of board members (herself included) and consultants. Together, this team agreed that they would apply best practices in aggressive project management, multi-loop feedback and coaching, and systemic organizational development analysis.

After a rapid diagnosis of the situation, the team constructed a wall-sized, colorful project map to mount in Limon's office. This would serve as a guide to the orientation and on-boarding process. The project map displayed a sequence of what Limon and team determined to be key action steps—seven of them, to be exact:

1. The corporate strategy and expectations for business and financial performance
2. The sales strategy and targets for the middle market
3. Sales management personnel at multiple levels
4. Newly hired sales representatives
5. Internal sales partners
6. Sky International as a cultural whole
7. Project management.

Thus chartered, Limon's project team next worked on creating a number of important guideposts, which they would align with predetermined best practices and implement for (let's hope) flawless execution. Next, they established a set of project team ground rules dictating the manner in which members would conduct themselves (they were expected to demonstrate respect and commitment to each other, complete aggressively timed work outputs, and meet all milestones).

The team then turned their attention to creating a list of design principles for the project. Regardless of the directives and methods they would decide upon, they knew that the orientation program would have to include the following four components:

1. Learning and performance outcomes for the newly hired sales representatives
2. Desired characteristics of the new sales culture
3. Sales performance metrics to track progress—tied to specific learning activities that produce important leading or lagging indicators within their market
4. Integrated in-class and in-field learning, feedback, and coaching.

The team envisioned the end result of the project to include a new sales force of licensed, certified sales representatives who would achieve specific, measurable performance at each stage of the middle-market sales cycle. Preferably, the sales force would achieve these performance levels within six months after the completion of the orientation program's curriculum.

Based on the established milestones and outcomes—and with the colorful project map used as a guide—the team created a comprehensive launch plan. The launch plan incorporated the design principles, Sky's project success criteria, and opportunities for managing positive defining moments or experiences for all participants. Scores of sequenced, detailed action steps with all tasks, accountabilities, and milestones guided the day-to-day activity.

Once the plan was in motion, the project team would meet twice weekly to review progress on these tasks, accountabilities, and milestones. Limon and the team all felt that these meetings—guided by the launch plan document— were especially valuable to the program's success. It made the task of managing the project and keeping the aggressive schedule all the more organized and visual.

But the team wasn't just looking at a document to keep themselves on task. They also relied upon Sky's comprehensive, internal communications plan— adapted for the sales team orientation project, of course. The communications plan highlighted the key characteristics of the new sales culture, underscored the compelling business case and urgent need for meeting or exceeding sales and financial performance metrics, and kept all key players fully informed of the accelerated development plan. Each stream of the communication plan was aligned to fit the cultural model of each role within the company and step within the orientation project. Limon and the other members of the senior management team were to receive formal progress reports from key players in the orientation team on a regular basis.

For these progress reports, project data were collected and openly shared. With these numbers at hand, the team would then work toward identifying and clarifying strategic links, writing custom learning designs and exercises, examining the degree of alignment among sales processes and systems, determining appropriate performance metrics, and uncovering cultural habits that could either inhibit or propel the intended learning and performance of the new sales force.

As a result of all their labors, the view from the ground floor was certainly sunny. From the very beginning—when all new hires reported for a two-day orientation to the business and sales process—glowing reviews were handed out all across the board.

As Limon would say, this happened for good reason: the program started off on the right foot. The initial two days of orientation were designed to be celebratory in nature, high energy, and fast paced. This tone and style was especially useful because it reflected the branding that was set forth in the recruitment and selection process, to say nothing of the expected employee experience. In effect, the first two days of the program deliberately demonstrated Sky's unique Employee Value Proposition.

Senior management from nearly all functions participated in the initial orientation sessions. From their respective roles, they described the organization's history, structure, and approach to the marketplace. They revealed (in great detail) the explicit new business strategy to re-enter the middle market. Every senior manager drew clear connections to create line of sight between the individuals in the new hire group and the targeted results. They regularly referenced Sky's version of the Triple Win for the organization, its intermediary sales channel, and its end customers.

Perhaps most importantly, Sky's management and training team exposed the operating model for how the organization makes money. Among the lessons:

- The sales channel
- The end customers
- Cultural values and expectations for performance
- The market structure
- Profitability formulas
- Business opportunities by segment
- The workforce trends that drive customer decisions
- Product and service trends
- The competitive environment
- Financial management and control.

At the end of each segment, the new hires were told that they would be receiving significantly more detail in all of these areas throughout the remainder of the 100-day on-boarding process.

Throughout days one and two, each new hire was openly told why they were selected for this unique assignment. With that in mind, the project team also laid out specific expectations for performance—expectations that had been carefully calculated and prepared in conjunction with sales and financial analysis. From an executive standpoint, these expectations were critically important for two reasons. First, the performance of the new hires on the pre-established business metrics would justify the sales strategy. Second, the performance would also gauge the return on invested capital in the new sales structure (and the Human Capital Cycle as a whole).

The evaluation methodology included a series of performance gates. At the close of each of five on-boarding sessions, the sales representatives would be required to complete mastery tests for technical, sales, and product knowledge and skills. In order to move on to the next session, the participant had to demonstrate a score of at least 70 percent score on the first try. In the case of re-testing, they needed to score at least an 85 percent. Failure to do so required remedial action and close work with an assigned coach. Other performance gates included completion of on-boarding seminar quality checklists and participant attitude questionnaires.

The project team also completed military-style after action reviews and training effectiveness action planning at the close of each of the five on-boarding sessions. Brief reviews of the findings were conducted each day. Then, at the end of each week, the team conducted a formal review of the progress with specific notations on milestones. They also scrutinized and further analyzed the competency scoring data.

A set of in-field guides were created to direct the new hires during each of the five-week cycles of on-boarding classroom curriculum. One half of the set would be given to the new hire and the other half to his/her manager. The intent was to provide structured learning on the business and customers, practical application of skills acquired in the previous session, and investigation into situations that would be objects of learning in the next session. As the on-boarding process progressed, more and more of the in-field guide incorporated learning and skill reinforcement from earlier sessions. This way, anything that may have served as a source of struggle for any of the sales representatives in the early weeks could be practiced and reinforced continually, thereby building competence, confidence, and comfort in the new skills and role.

Early anecdotal and leading indicator evidence emerged within a few weeks after the completion on the on-boarding process. Within the next year, the team reported a double-digit improvement in performance on the given milestones and metrics. Limon knew that this meant her company had received a clear return on investment in human capital.

As a result of the successful launch of this new sales force, Sky International chose to offer future on-boarding in a similar pattern. It also examined how such a process might be adapted for other functional areas and to provide a source of ongoing learning and development for current sales force groups in other business units.

SUMMARY

Employee on-boarding and orientation may seem like a convoluted process. It is certainly complicated and time-consuming. But if an organization's senior management takes the time to ensure that the key steps outlined in this chapter are met, the orientation process will be a raging success—and the company, with its highly talented, highly motivated new workforce, will be that much closer to achieving a Triple Win.

The key steps for a successful on-boarding and orientation process are the following:

1. Link each employee role to its corresponding strategic outcome
2. Establish specific expectations for roles, responsibilities, and standards of performance
3. Demonstrate the Employee Value Proposition
4. Equip new employees with essential knowledge about the organization, its customers, and its partners
5. Connect new hires to people from whom they can learn
6. Provide network maps of people
7. Facilitate a learning environment in which employees can feel comfortable.

8

DEVELOPMENT OF ONGOING CAPABILITIES OR CAREER GROWTH

T HE NEXT STAGE of the Human Capital Cycle focuses on the development of ongoing capabilities or the career growth of employees. It begins shortly after a new employee embarks upon the initial on-boarding and orientation process. This stage is different from the others, given that it could take anywhere from several months to several decades to reach its natural conclusion. This being the case, the development of ongoing capabilities or career growth absorbs the most time, attention, and resources of all stages within the Human Capital Cycle.

This stage typically comes with a set of significant assumptions. First, it can be assumed that most organizations will conduct a periodic business review of some depth prior to formulating its career growth plan. The review could include points similar to the key tasks proposed in the emergence of new need/ strategy stage. Ideally, the focal point of this stage should be on the review by the senior management team and the definition of the Human Capital Plan requirements to fulfill business ambitions.

A second major assumption is that multiple developmental processes will be in motion at any given time. Examples may include:

- A strategy to build leadership
- A plan to determine all successor candidates
- A measurement of critical performer bench strength
- A boost in capability, securing greater competitive advantage
- A call to each employee to maintain professional certifications and licensure.

The final assumption is that the programs for development will draw from a broad spectrum of styles and settings. Among these styles and settings:

- Individual to large group learning
- Traditional classroom sessions

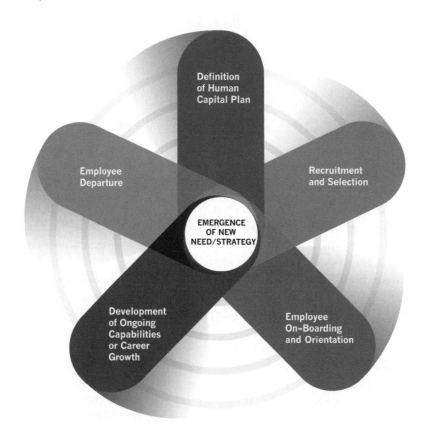

- Technology-driven learning
- One-on-one peer mentoring
- Global conferences
- Simple memorization on the part of the employee
- In-field action learning
- Real-time innovation.

The Human Capital Cycle remains relatively neutral on the choice of learning methodologies. It instead insists on a thoughtful choice that fits the needs of the learner as well as the organization.

In many cases, when it comes to career growth, organizations fall short of their Human Capital needs simply because they pick what they believe to be the simplest and most logical way to foster their employees along a reasonable career track. They see that vacancies have been created by departing members of the leadership or critical talent pool and they work to promote from within.

In a separate survey question, respondents to the poll of 307 American business and government leaders ranked the importance of skills necessary to advance to higher level leadership positions.[1] Those with a ranking of "important/very important" are shown in Figure 8.1.

What is interesting about the survey rankings shown below is that they are quite consistent with findings from another executive leadership research study conducted by Stephen Zaccaro.[2] Through his research (and the research of many others), Zaccaro has come to the conclusion that, in the past, there seems to have been a high level of focus upon conceptual or cognitive skills when choosing people to promote up the ladder of a given organization. The focus on technical skills within the functional area from which these people were drawn was modest, at best.

Today, however, that paradigm has shifted. What Zaccaro and others have found in recent studies is that the demand for exceptional social skills or interpersonal skills lies about equal with the call for conceptual skills. Technical skills, it seems, are very much on the rise.

The results of the AchieveGlobal survey showed that 75 percent of respondents had promoted up to 25 percent of their high-potential candidates since the inception of their Human Capital program. Another 18 percent had promoted between 26 percent and 50 percent of such candidates. Only 7 percent had promoted more than half of their high-potential people (HPs), as shown in Figure 8.2.

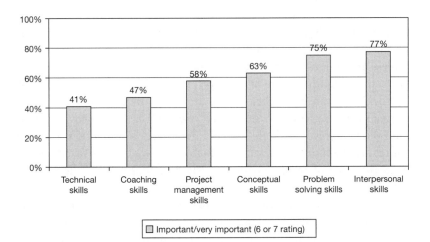

Figure 8.1

Importance of Skills Needed to Advance to Higher Leadership Positions

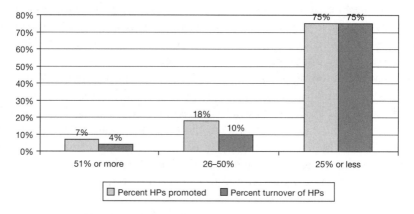

Figure 8.2
Rate of High Potential Promotions and Turnover

Figure 8.2 is significant for one reason: unless an organization is willing to lose some of its best performers, it is critically important that it makes the effort to track the progress of these individuals as well as research the proper timeframe under which to promote them.

The senior management team needs to be careful with how it approaches the issues of prospective performance and the timeframe of promotions. If candidates are informed of their position within the company as a high-potential employee, they tend to construe this designation as a form of promise for promotion (kind of a *quasi*-contract). This is fine until it comes time to fill a position within the company that would represent a promotion for these individuals. Typically, if high-potential performers are passed over for a higher position, they feel cheated and disappointed, and tend to build up contempt.

Unless an effort to communicate intent on the part of the senior management team (or another more direct superior) is made—unless some measure of reconciliation can be reached—there are surely ramifications in employee performance and retention to be expected. Remember, it does not matter if an organization promises its high-potential employees a promotion; the simple act of telling them of their status as a high-level employee is usually enough to make that offer of promotion implicit. They *will* misconstrue the intentions.

This loss of employees due to oversight is typically compounded by the fact that, most often, executive teams don't look to their own high-potential people right away when they are making their placement decisions. As often as not, the search for this ideal candidate is done outside the organization.

Career growth is perhaps the most important stage of the Human Capital Cycle because it is the one that ensures talented people stick with the organization for longer. It also helps to foster a sense of accomplishment and fulfillment for these talented people—which of course boosts productivity, efficiency, and morale. With a staff of talented people performing well, an organization is sure to experience the Triple Win. Revenue increases, expenses decrease, market share is gained, and public perception of the organization improves.

GOALS AND OUTCOMES

The list of desired outcomes for the career growth stage is a natural reflection of the assumptions appearing above. Before getting into the goals and outcomes, however, it would be prudent to outline the two facets of developing ongoing capabilities in a new staff. One facet is short-term learning and the other is long-term learning.

The short-term response typically involves a set of seminars designed to build a narrowly focused skill or capability. Conversely, the long-term response involves either a comprehensive organizational learning map (to accommodate the ongoing capabilities of multiple career paths), a multi-college university curriculum, or an annually updated learning strategy applied to the organization on a global scale.

Regardless of the approach, the successful organization is the one that subscribes to the following key tasks.

CONTINUALLY PREPARE AND INFORM ALL MEMBERS OF THE ORGANIZATION

The ultimate goal of the Human Capital Cycle is to generate and retain as much critical knowledge and talent as possible. That being the case, the ongoing development stage is only as effective as its leaders are prepared. It is clear that the most direct line to developing critical talent is to incorporate existing critical talent into the fold. In order to facilitate the most effective career growth stage, it is important that all members in a decision making role are informed of the overarching organizational strategy.

PROVIDE OUTLETS FOR CONTINUED GROWTH AND DEVELOPMENT OF CURRENT AND NEW SKILLS

The first and most obvious outlet for this outcome is to build a curriculum that allows for continued education and development throughout the career cycle.

The case has already been made for the use of a competency-based approach for recruitment and selection, but this approach has the added benefit of organizing the principles of the developmental curriculum. For example, competency-based training that contains structured skill practices has a tendency to shift the on-the-job performance curve 0.7 standard deviations and produce a 700 percent return on investment. This approach also produces almost two times the improvement in performance and eight times the return of investment in training (when that training focuses on theory and knowledge acquisition).[3]

The development process, however, should be defined as far more than just standard classroom, online, or blended learning. It should include deep experience and learning from peers and mentors. In order to create social and developmental connections, the senior management team should consider providing critical knowledge and talent performers with the tools and guidance they need to build networks. These connections can enhance individual and organizational performance and also improve the quality of their personal interactions with others.

ALIGN HUMAN CAPITAL CAPABILITIES WITH THE STRATEGIC NEEDS OF THE ORGANIZATION

Perhaps the most effective way to organize the content within the Human Capital Cycle is to identify the competency set that best serves the current business strategy. Organizations are more successful and effective (in a business sense) if they begin the competency identification process with the critical knowledge and talent that drives the Customer Value Proposition.

A valuable form of business intelligence can be found by tracing the application of critical knowledge and talent to the impact of development strategies. This creates a visible line of sight from the business strategy, to the critical knowledge and talent, to the aligned development or learning strategy, to the application of newly acquired knowledge and skill, and finally to the business impact or results produced. This process provides the organization with information that serves as an important foundation in strategic decision making. It also manages Human Capital and sets a clear direction for the future of the organization.

FAIRLY AND EFFICIENTLY IDENTIFY NEW CAREER GROWTH OPPORTUNITIES

Many times, the organization that does not experience career growth among its employees is the organization that does not make it clear where growth opportunities exist. This clarity cuts both ways. Without research into the company's strengths and weaknesses (on an organizational, customer, and employee scale), executives and other people in a position of leadership will not recognize where they need to be concentrating their efforts on generating growth.

Furthermore, unless employees (particularly talented individuals) are made aware of their opportunities to expand their acumen and thus advance their careers, their track will stagnate and they will lose interest. Loss of interest leads to any number of undesirable things. Among them: a drop in productivity, a decline in employee morale, and a loss of otherwise talented employees—all of which contributes to a negative impact on business effectiveness.

PROVIDE EMPLOYEES WITH THE INITIATIVE TO GROW AND CONTRIBUTE

It is one thing to ask an employee to focus on career growth and development. It is entirely another to give the employee incentive to do so. Whether that incentive is monetary in nature is up to the senior management team, but in any case, there needs to be a systematic intervention on employee motivation.

Even if monetary rewards are established, programs such as these have a tendency to pay for themselves. For example, AchieveGlobal conducted extensive testing of a leadership development program with performance-based instructional design—as well as skills practice and reinforcement. Comparing the results before and after the training for both trained and control groups, a 336 percent return on investment was reported.

Many organizations have gained greater Human Capital benefits by focusing their ongoing development agenda on varying degrees of participative management, as well. According to an intensive study of management practices of Fortune 1,000 companies, the Center for Effective Organizations at the University of Southern California found that significant use of employee involvement practices such as information sharing, skills training, rewards programs, and empowerment efforts produced important results. These included the following:

- A return on sales increase of 66 percent
- A return on assets increase of 20 percent
- A return on investment increase of 20 percent
- A higher return on equity of 13 percent.

These results suggest that a minimum of some level of collaboration or increased involvement in ongoing development curricula was incorporated.[4] And the returns speak for themselves.

CONTINUE TO FACILITATE THE EMPLOYEE VALUE PROPOSITION

Again, the Employee Value Proposition is essentially the lifeblood of any successful employee recruitment and retention process. The Human Capital Cycle is no different. Without the clear and ongoing presentation of the EVP, employees will begin to lose sight of why they chose the organization they currently work for in the first place. Unless the EVP remains visible, all other tasks and outcomes become irrelevant.

All six of these outcomes may seem broad and long term, but part of the beauty of the Human Capital Cycle is that it incorporates these new practices in organizational culture. In the long run, organizations may sit back and watch their talented people experience fulfilling career growth as they work efficiently and effectively to benefit the Triple Win.

HEALTHY CAREER GROWTH

When the National Partnership for Reinventing Government was challenged to provide better service to the American public by using tax dollars more efficiently and effectively, the federal landscape began to change. One health service division within a federal agency (we will call it Health Initiative) decided to heed the call by focusing on bringing in and developing more talented people. To meet this measure, it turned to a competency-based leadership development curriculum.

Health Initiative began by defining and crystallizing the desired outcome of its Human Capital Plan: "To maintain a work environment that encourages creativity, diversity, innovation, teamwork, and the highest ethical standard." But even with the outcome in mind, the agency still needed to develop a culture across many functions and geographic regions if it hoped to be ready for effective, results-oriented management. In the midst of this challenge, the agency also needed to develop and support a highly skilled, diverse, and committed workforce.

So its next step was to conduct a nationwide survey designed to identify those employees who would gain the greatest benefit from appropriate leadership skills development. The primary audience? First-time leaders.

Having identified its new potential leaders, Health Initiative then tailored a curriculum to include leadership skill building (all skills matching the agency's core values) as well as important policy and job-related information. The curriculum was then passed on to the instructors, who in turn launched the program at several locations across the United States.

Three years later, the agency chose to test the effectiveness of the training. To meet that end, it secured the services of AchieveGlobal, who conducted a Kirkpatrick Level 3 evaluation of observed behavior change. The evaluation process included hundreds of training participants and their colleagues from across five separate sites.

Behavioral observation data was collected in five categories:

1. The training participant's effectiveness in applying the thirty pre-established leadership skills required for the new culture
2. The performance of the employees who reported regularly to the participant
3. The job satisfaction of the training participant
4. The onsite work climate
5. The effectiveness of the training over the three-year period.

The conclusions drawn from these data were favorable. The average post-training scores for all thirty skill items or leadership behaviors were consistently, substantially, and significantly higher than pre-training scores. The employees of the managers who completed the training exhibited a statistically significant increase in their level of performance —and they were better equipped to manage their own employees' performance, as well. All across the board, improvements in leadership skills abound; improvements such as communications, decision making, and change management. Finally, in each of the sites, participants demonstrated an ability to determine how to work more effectively.

By fulfilling the evaluation process, Health Initiative was able to demonstrate a significant improvement in its Human Capital capabilities. And better yet, it began to use its funding more efficiently and effectively, in accordance with the decree from the National Partnership for Reinventing Government.[5]

HOW TO DEVELOP ONGOING CAPABILITIES AND PROMOTE CAREER GROWTH

The key tasks of this stage are arguably the most important of any key task in the Human Capital Cycle. This is because their completion ensures a focused, productive, happy, and long-term employee and leadership base. These key tasks include many of the standard requirements to develop ongoing capabilities or career growth.

STEP 1: IDENTIFY THE COMPETENCIES REQUIRED OF CRITICAL TALENT PERFORMERS

Within most organizations, there are many roles that must be filled. In some cases, the roles are vacant because of the departure of a highly talented individual. In other cases, the role is currently occupied by someone who has the potential to grow into a better performer. And in other cases, the role is occupied by someone who could and should be replaced by a high-level performer who has demonstrated a track of exceptional career growth.

Regardless of the case, the senior management team must conduct a careful and thorough assessment of the competencies required of its talented performers. Each organization is unique, but for the most part, talented performers all have a few traits in common. In addition to that, employees are more likely to grow confidently and effectively if they already possess a majority of the following characteristics:

- Ability to perform the core task for their roles
- Self-disciplined
- Goal-directed
- Flexible
- Collaborative
- Willing to share and exchange information
- Open to feedback, change, differences in people and culture, ways of thinking, other discipline models or signature skills, and alternative approaches to processes
- Committed and connected to the business
- Competent in using the technology required for their roles.[6]

The organization that selects and trains individuals meeting the above criteria will experience the greatest return on its career growth agenda.

This stage will recommend the application of group environments in order to facilitate career growth across the board. With that being the case, it is important that the organization selects for individuals who thrive in such an environment. It is also recommended that the above characteristics be considered when identifying ongoing developmental opportunities.

STEP 2: CONDUCT PERIODIC ASSESSMENT OF CAPABILITIES AND GROWTH—COMPARE WITH CHANGING ORGANIZATIONAL NEEDS

No company operates in a vacuum. No organization is stagnant in its growth or staffing needs. Because of this fact, it is important to take the time (on a regular basis) to assess the capabilities and growth of the employee pool.

The active engagement and growth process of the critical knowledge and talent performers is critical to this step—but unfortunately, a relatively small percentage of organizations are viewed as effective in this aspect of ongoing development. For example, in a survey of nearly 8,000 global business executives conducted by *The McKinsey Quarterly* in June, 2005, only 27 percent of the respondents stated that their organizations were effective at matching talent with opportunities. This perceived condition creates frustration for managers, who are urgently seeking talent, and eager employees, who are searching for growth.

But with the application of this stage of the Human Capital Cycle, many organizations are now conducting periodic assessments of capabilities and then comparing the current status with the ever-changing needs of the organization. Ongoing capability development is being instituted through global talent reviews. And employee populations are better assessed in every country, function, and business under organizational management.

The most successful organizations use these periodic assessments to uncover their respective capacities to find, develop, deploy, engage, and retain skilled people. They also evaluate the success rate of key promotions by using quantitative and qualitative measures (a process that typically covers a three-year period).[7]

STEP 3: PROVIDE COACHING, FEEDBACK, REINFORCEMENT, AND RECOGNITION OF GROWTH

The employee that does not see his/her progress is the employee that leaves the firm. Career growth is obviously critical to any successful Human Capital agenda, but it is not possible if the growth is not measured, reinforced, and demonstrated to the employee. With coaching, the employee can be guided toward career growth as the organization sees fit. With reinforcement, morale remains high on the task of developing ongoing capabilities. And with recognition of growth, the employee may see the progress that he/she has made on the process—and won't wind up feeling like he/she is flailing at something that the organization has deemed important.

The result? More productive people, a healthier bottom line, and happier customers.

STEP 4: CONDUCT FORMAL AND INFORMAL PERFORMANCE MANAGEMENT

Performance management, on both fronts, is designed to help the organization to assess how its employees are doing on their career growth curve on a regular basis. Data must be gathered and continuing upkeep of the strategy must be performed.

The reason for this is simple: people's learning curves have a tendency to do just that—curve. Even for highly talented performers, the concentrated focus on career growth tends to align with what has been described as "summit syndrome." In a classic S-curve (or Sigmoidal curve), high performers quickly show promise and ascend within the organization quite noticeably. These superstars often engage avidly in learning and developing. The syndrome becomes apparent only when the ascendancy peaks, at which point the performer's edge softens.

In other words, even for an organization's most highly talented individuals, the performance on career growth tends to plateau. Most of the time, this is because the performer finds him/herself frequently confused by and distracted from career focus and performance. This decrease in performance can lead to career-limiting behaviors of all sorts.

To keep performers on track, Step 3 is certainly helpful. Career assessment, guidance, and mentoring are all helpful practices. Pair this with performance management practices—and a healthy dose of managerial objectivity—and these lapses in performance can be avoided.[8]

STEP 5: CREATE A TALENT MARKET TO ACCELERATE GROWTH

One emerging approach, especially for critical knowledge and talent performer development through job rotation, is the creation of an internal talent market. Instead of relying on only upper-level management to identify rotation opportunities and candidates (a classic "push" mentality), the talent market provides a more fluid, inclusive, and self-directed "pull" approach that tends to attract a greater number of people.

This shift requires the attention of the senior management team as well as all Human Resources staff members, as they will typically operate as market makers when it comes time to formalize and manage the process of talent market development. When all is said and done, the HR team will prepare descriptions of opportunities and talent profiles, screen applications, adjudicate standards and protocols, and ensure equitable due process.

Many would say that an informal, internal talent market works well in professional services—whether academic or research and development—but only when there are fewer than a hundred participants. It is not impossible for larger companies to create an internal talent market, however. Larger, more complex global organizations such as American Express and IBM have formalized these talent markets. In their cases, they use them for the efficient placement of junior and mid-level professionals.[9]

STEP 6: RECONCILE ACTIONS WITHIN TALENT MANAGEMENT AND SUCCESSION PLANNING

Obviously, the development of ongoing capabilities is most effective when it leads to real solutions for the organization in danger of losing its best performers. The Human Capital Cycle calls for considerable research into the organization's talent management and succession planning needs because the senior management team cannot hope to gain anything useful from its career growth plan until it knows exactly what kind of career growth is needed.

So in other words, the development of ongoing capabilities needs to be brought in line with the expected departure of key employees. If there are at least a few highly talented individuals training on the skills necessary to assume the job of a departing high-level manager, then succession planning from within the organization becomes that much simpler to conduct.

STEP 7: COMMUNICATE DEVELOPMENTAL OPPORTUNITIES AND PROCESS FOR PARTICIPATION

This communication must be conducted at all levels—from the top down. Everyone from the CEO to the Human Resources team to seasoned employees to the pool of new hires must be made aware of the opportunities for career growth and the process for participating in that growth. A career growth track is far more effective if everyone is nudged in the right direction, after all.

Together, all seven of these steps lead to a cohesive, effective, and cost-efficient whole. Employees will find themselves more motivated and willing to participate in ongoing career development and staff will be more efficient at the delivery of that development. Clarity will be reached by the executive team, bonds will be formed between employees, and most importantly, high-level performers will be far more likely to stick around for the long term.

CAREER GROWTH AT WORK

Even before it began expanding its drafting and sales departments to enter a new market, Sky International already possessed significant financial strength and a coveted reputation for quality of product and customer relations across the board. Still, Limon and the rest of the senior management team chose to study how they might bring the company to an even higher level of performance—how they might best maintain the accelerated growth trajectory they had experienced during the condo boom.

Having already effectively studied the need for a shift in strategic direction, carefully conducted analysis of its capabilities, and determined to undertake an enterprise-wide development strategy, Sky was soon able to provide the basis for how the entire enterprise might engage in an even more aggressive growth path.

But Limon understood that growth can be maintained only if valuable employees are retained. So she began to look into the creation of an internal "university" to support the company's primary business segments. The university would be set up to align with the talent management process that had already been implemented across the organization. All curricula at this university would be competency focused to meet the needs of each individual business segment. In addition, Limon and the executive board would establish a core curricula that would allow for movement across the organization by key leaders and critical talent performers, should the need arise.

To help facilitate these career growth and continuing development needs, Limon ordered exploratory research into the demographics of Sky International. Among the trends and data, she and her executive team discovered important insights for managing the careers of critical knowledge and talent performers. Seven key characteristics were found among the insights. Critical knowledge and talent performers:

- Know their worth or market value
- Have the organizational savvy necessary to identify who holds key resources and how to successfully gravitate to them
- Tend to ignore corporate hierarchy

- Expect unencumbered, instant access to C-suite decision makers
- Stay well connected with highly active knowledge networks
- Demonstrate a low threshold for boredom
- Prefer not to be led by a boss, but rather, by a "benevolent guardian."[10]

With the typical critical talent performer identified, Limon and her team could focus their efforts on determining how to facilitate ongoing development for such highly demanding and refined employees. What they decided was that one cannot train a critical talent performer in the same way that one can train just any low-level employee. High-potential employees must be exposed to the full range of business activities. The so-called "higher impact" opportunities would include the following:

- Managing large groups
- Launching and implementing major initiatives, programs, or even new businesses
- Applying significant decision making or governance authority
- Working with other functions on collaborative or action learning teams
- Performing in customer-facing roles
- Leading a critical turn-around situation.[11]

Like any building ever constructed by Sky International, Limon's plan would not be complete without a sound support structure. Her research into the subject of ongoing career growth had uncovered that the most successful programs are those that employ peer mentors.

So the executives at Sky knew that they could not launch their new operating model without including peer mentoring in their development program. The role of peer mentors would be to help their peers expand and apply new skills, knowledge, and capabilities over the long term of their lives with the company. Limon, thanks to the mentoring program, could expect the new hires to gain confidence and comfort when navigating the organizational culture in the throes of the operating changes. With the mentoring relationship serving as a safe haven for open dialogue, she could also expect a more thorough stream of constructive feedback and coaching from non-management sources (something that tends to shed far more light on organizational challenges, issues, and concerns than management reporting alone).

But Limon knew she wasn't finished yet. She still had to determine the characteristics of a perfect peer mentor. She couldn't simply line up all ten-year veterans of the organization and expect them to be the ideal mentors for all incoming new hires. So in order to model the perfect candidates, she developed the list that follows. The ideal peer mentor:

- Resides in convenient geographic proximity and accessibility to the mentee
- Has the opportunity to regularly observe the mentee in action
- Demonstrates a consistent track record of performance and positive relationships
- Has in-depth understanding and working knowledge of the operating model and related skills
- Knows the economics of the business and the connections with performance metrics, processes, and roles of other players
- Demonstrates superior communications and interpersonal skills, especially in giving constructive feedback, providing recognition, and coaching
- Exhibits a consistent motivation and personal satisfaction in assisting and developing others
- Exercises initiative with positive results
- Has a reputation for easily establishing a relationship based on mutual trust and respect
- Fosters a positive coaching environment.

As Limon would soon discover, peer mentoring serves an extremely valuable role in this stage of the Human Capital Cycle. This is because not only does it help make the new hire feel more comfortable, but also it fosters career growth in *both* the mentor and the mentee. It is also particularly effective in that it helps to spread critical knowledge and talent from employee to employee.

SUMMARY

The development of ongoing capabilities stage is certainly a continuous one. It requires the most consistent attention on the part of the senior management team—and in particular, the chief human capital officers. But the time and effort tends to pay off in spades. The company who keeps its employees motivated and loyal often finds the most Triple Win success.

In summary, here are the steps to ensure this outcome:

1. Identify the competencies required of critical talent performers
2. Conduct periodic assessment of capabilities and growth—compare with changing organizational needs
3. Provide coaching, feedback, reinforcement, and recognition of growth
4. Conduct formal and informal performance management
5. Create a talent market to accelerate growth
6. Reconcile actions within talent management and succession planning
7. Communicate developmental opportunities and process for participation.

Chapter

9

EMPLOYEE DEPARTURE

T HE FINAL STAGE of the Human Capital Cycle focuses on the difficult and delicate topic of employee departure. Given the variability of this inevitable event, this stage includes a broad array of topics. But there are a few in particular that warrant a deeper look. The organization that knows where its critical knowledge and talent may be at risk will be able to better plan for its sustainment. It is also remarkably effective at engaging workers beyond the normal retirement period.

There are certainly other strategies and agendas to consider, but in the end, the most important thing for a company is to understand the rationale and full cost of employee turnover.

Research data strengthens the case for paying special attention to this final stage of the cycle. A massive wave of retirement is already underway. Although variations in economic cycles may dampen this effect in the short term, the inventory of critical knowledge and talent is already shifting and declining. In some industries, growth ambitions and service to customers and constituents has been curtailed by significant talent shortages. The labor market is becoming more competitive in unexpected ways. The cost of turnover continues to escalate—and carries a far-reaching impact on an organization and its customers. And worst of all, employees are acting on their restlessness and dissatisfaction or disenchantment with greater frequency.

In addition to the troubling statistics already presented, consider the following key data points:

- Consensus among hiring and HR managers is that departments and organizations are challenged with low employee morale and issues with knowledge transfer and deterioration of employee relationships due to severe attrition.[1]
- The probability that an employee will leave due to a lack of growth and development opportunities is 36 percent. The probability that employees will leave due to unfair treatment is 25 percent.[2]

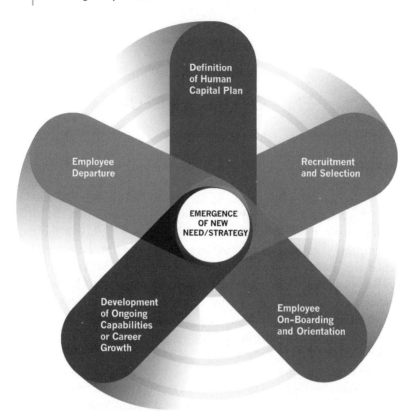

This kind of turnover negatively effects an organization in more ways than understaffing, as well. Consider Figure 9.1.

As Figure 9.1 demonstrates, employee turnover has a significantly negative impact on many aspects of an organization, the impact being most severe on employee morale and knowledge transfer, but even having some limted impact on community relations at the lower end of the scale. Each of these issues directly influences a company's ability to improve revenues, decrease expenses, and gain market share, as well. This being the case, it is critically important that an organization pay heed to the goals and outcomes that follow.

GOALS AND OUTCOMES

Employees leave for any number of reasons. Some times, their departures are planned and can be accounted for in advance. Other times, the departures are premature and come as a surprise to everyone involved. Any form of departure affects the organization, its customers, and all employees, but

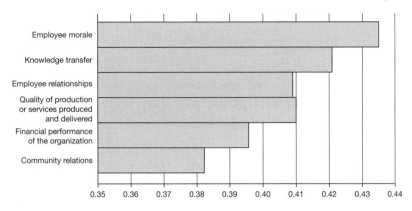

Figure 9.1
Impact Reported by Managers Indicating How Turnover Negatively Affected Their
Organization (Negative Impact Index for U.S., Asia, and European Regions)

the overarching outcome of this stage is to sustain the critical knowledge
and talent that the organization needs in order to continue achieving prime
business results.

SUSTAIN ORGANIZATIONAL KNOWLEDGE AND TALENT

This is the primary outcome for good reason. The knowledge and talent that
an organization possesses is the very thing that makes that organization work.
Without the sustainment of organizational knowledge and talent, it cannot
expect to sustain the benefits it has for so long provided to its customers.

ACHIEVE ORDERLY, RESPECTFUL, AND DIGNIFIED CLOSURE TO EACH EMPLOYEE'S CAREER

Disgruntled former employees can be damaging in more ways than one. For
one thing, they tend to contribute to lowering employee morale, whether
operating inside or outside the organization. For another, they tend to be far
more motivated to contribute knowledge and talent to their new employers—
employers that may be competitors to the organization they have just vacated.
In this way, it is essential that all employees, regardless of whether they are
leaving on good or bad terms, are made to understand their value before they
walk out the door. There are simple strategies to bring orderly, respectful, and
dignified closure to the career of any employee—but the importance of this
outcome cannot be underemphasized.

FIND CLARITY ON THE RATIONALE FOR ALL EMPLOYEE DEPARTURES

Information is key to any agenda in business. Employee departure is no exception. The more the organization knows about why its employees are leaving, the quicker the senior management team can resolve the problems that lead to the departure in the first place.

PROMOTE A POSITIVE REPUTATION FOR THE ORGANIZATION

Nobody wants to work for an organization with a negative reputation. That reputation can come from the marketplace or within the organization's own walls. Unless the organization takes strides to improve its reputation to the point where it is known to be a good organization to work for, it can expect to see regular and damaging employee departure.

FOLLOW-THROUGH ON THE EMPLOYEE VALUE PROPOSITION

By now, it should be quite clear that the Employee Value Proposition is the central element to the Human Capital Cycle. Even though this stage deals with employees at or on their way out, the EVP is just as important here as it is in any other stage.

The importance of critical knowledge and talent has been emphasized throughout the discussion of the Human Capital Cycle, as well. Organizational performance and competitive advantage depend highly on the maximization and return on this resource—it is after all the source that delivers the greatest value at the core of the business mission. The organization that achieves the above outcomes winds up keeping more of its critical knowledge and talent performers than its competitors. And this always leads to greater success in the respective market.

A CRITICAL LOSS

What can occur if this stage of the Human Capital Cycle is not watched carefully? For one thing, the company that ignores it might be headed for a rather sobering experience. Consider Matthew Jeffries, President of PaperPack Incorporated. With growing consumer awareness of environmental issues, several customers had expressed the need for more environmentally-friendly options, and were considering whether or not to renew their contracts for PaperPack's core packaging products.

Faced with the possibility of the company's core products becoming increasingly less viable, Jeffries called together the rest of the senior management team. Deep, strategic discussions ensued. A number of prudent management actions were settled upon, and the new strategy was enacted.

Investments were needed in R&D to ramp up the company's range of "green" products, and further down the line, more cash would be needed to re-tool existing manufacturing plants. In order to free-up the required resources Jeffries and his CFO focused on where to cut expenses. In so doing, they unknowingly triggered the loss of a number of talented performers.

One of the many targets of cost-saving opportunities included a tighter rein on the payroll cost of two departments. The senior team also looked at the comparative time provided in customer service interactions.

Despite the planned intentions, the instructions for the change cascaded throughout the management chain and ultimately produced unintended consequences. Messages to a number of talented people were delivered as warnings to watch the amount of time and attention given to customers. Unfortunately, several of the talented performers mistakenly considered the messages to be performance notices—they thought that maybe they were being reprimanded for improper work ethic. Given that they were such talented performers, they were understandably miffed.

Asked to do more with less, a number of other talented performers quickly became exhausted. As a result, discretionary effort began to dissolve. Employees began sharing feelings of contempt—discussing the issue as if they had been punished. Varying degrees of disengagement followed. Employees who had previously ignored the hordes of recruiters knocking on their door on a weekly basis now began to listen. One by one, the core of top performers left.

Finally, the senior management team got the message. Fortunately for Jeffries, things didn't get completely out of hand.

The consequences of ignoring this stage of the Human Capital Cycle can be incredibly significant. PaperPack could have lost every ounce of value generated by its talented performers. Business growth and customer loyalty could have suffered. An avalanche of departures by other employees—critically talented or otherwise—could have occurred if the low morale, adverse opinions, and observed injustices had been allowed to continue.

A few of the more significant consequences are as follows:

- Loss of critical knowledge and talent
- Measurable business shortfalls
- Failure to perform for customers
- The promotion of an unfavorable reputation for the organization
- The dissolving of the Employee Value Proposition
- The loss of other employees.

The moral of the story is that ignoring this stage of the Human Capital Cycle can be a catastrophic mistake. Organizations that pay attention only to the recruitment, selection, and training of new employees without worrying about employee departure are often headed for disaster.

HOW TO COPE WITH EMPLOYEE DEPARTURE

Every organization is strongly encouraged to understand which of its most talented performers fall within the window of either potential or planned retirements. In addition, it is important to assess the risk of losing highly talented people for other reasons such as recruitment by competing firms or simply low employee morale.

The organization that follows the steps below is the organization that properly assesses employee departure, prepares for it perfectly, and smoothly implements the process of replacing departed talent. It is also the organization that sees consistent improvement in the Triple Win.

STEP 1: ENGAGE IN A PERIODIC REVIEW OF CAPABILITIES AND IDENTIFY POSSIBLE DEPARTURES

It is important to note that evaluating each employee's likelihood to depart the company is not just a one-time analysis of birthdates on the employee roster. Not all employees depart at the age of 62. Some leave earlier for other companies. Some are recruited away. Some retire much earlier or much later. That being the case, it is critical that the organization conduct a thorough identification of the status of all mission critical performers.

For this task, the executive team must identify the names, roles, and locations of all talented performers. The departures could be for any reason—

not just retirement. And they should be tracked by a thorough examination of employee engagement and other cues of potential departure (such as a decline in productivity or responsiveness to tasks, for example). With these names in hand, the senior management team should then conduct an in-depth review of possible departures. The review should reveal a much deeper understanding of how employees are making choices about potential departures.

The end result of Step 1 is a clearer picture of the critical knowledge and talent that may be at risk. The senior management team might discover that one particular mission within the fold is at greater risk than another. And as a result, they may ramp up efforts to train or recruit replacements within that specific mission.

STEP 2: RECOGNIZE THE CONTRIBUTIONS OF THE DEPARTING EMPLOYEE TO THE MISSION AND VISION OF THE COMPANY

Rather than simply saying goodbye to departing employees with a handshake and a smile, the senior management team should also determine how they can expect to take a loss on productivity and value—and regardless of how good the training and recruiting strategy is, there will be at least a short-term loss in both. Knowing in advance what might happen upon losing a valuable employee tends to help mitigate most damages.

Further, this step helps begin the process of developing specific plans for preserving and circulating the remaining critical knowledge and talent.

STEP 3: ANALYZE RATIONALE FOR ALL TURNOVER—USE IT TO IMPROVE HUMAN CAPITAL PLANNING AT ALL STAGES

Employees will leave any organization for any number of reasons. It is not enough to assume that the turnover occurred simply because the employee(s) moved on to other things. Some organizations get into the pattern of hiring new employees out of college, only to watch them leave two years later. These organizations tend to chalk up their high rate of turnover to the idea that many of their new hires were just using them as springboards to other careers. Still other organizations turn a blind eye when the older of their members depart, assuming that it was all owed to retirement.

Unless the organization examines all employee turnover, valuable information will be lost. The most ideal resource for learning about why an employee has left the firm is the departing employee him/herself. The information that this person can provide can and should be used to improve all phases of the

Human Capital Cycle—and can even be used to bolster or revise the Employee Value Proposition.

STEP 4: ASSESS IMPACT OF POTENTIAL DEPARTURES ON THE ORGANIZATION AND CUSTOMERS

Preparation is always paramount when it comes to business—and in the case of Human Capital Management, there is no exception. The senior management team must take strides to determine exactly how much value the organization receives from all employees in danger of departing. Value cuts both ways. Losing a high-quality member of the team tends to decrease productivity, quality, and effectiveness for the organization. All of those declines tend to have a direct effect on what the customer can expect, as well.

Doing the due diligence on this task will not ensure that the decline in productivity and quality be avoided, but it will help mitigate it. Knowing what lies ahead on the road makes it far easier to avert crisis.

STEP 5: PLAN FOR THE EFFECTIVE TRANSFER OF KNOWLEDGE WITH OTHER DESIGNATED EMPLOYEES

With the preparation in hand—and with the understanding of what levels and kinds of knowledge might soon be departing—the team may then turn to determining ways to transfer that knowledge from the departing employee to his/her replacement.

To meet this end, some organizations are providing retraining opportunities to technical performers whose skill sets have not kept up with newer technologies. This allows those who have kept up to train and teach those who have not. Job sharing is another effective opportunity. If this concept is deployed with greater frequency, the loss of one employee does not necessarily mean the loss of an entire brand of knowledge.

The boomerang effect is something to watch out for, as well. Companies who offer financial incentives to employees who might be thinking about leaving retirement and returning to the workforce often find that they get back a few of the people they have lost. If not simply financial incentives, then it might benefit to trim the typical penalties of retirement, an act that usually makes it easier and more attractive for older, experienced people to return to work on a full-time or part-time basis.

Fortunately, for those organizations that are not sure where to look for experienced and critically talented employees, a new cottage industry of placement services has emerged. These placement services companies cater to people who have already left the labor market. More and more employers draw from their pools of retirees each year. The retirees who possess critical knowledge and talent and want to continue their life contributions are especially attractive to organizations in need.

STEP 6: MAINTAIN APPROPRIATE, ONGOING GOODWILL WITH DEPARTING AND REMAINING EMPLOYEES

The concept of gathering information from departing employees has already been mentioned. But it should also be known that keeping up with these employees once they are gone also has a tremendous effect. An organization that lets its departed employees know that it still cares about their wellbeing is far more likely to see that employee return. Sometimes, simply checking in on that employee gets the job done.

There are the remaining employees to consider, as well. Many of them will be left with the monumental task of picking up the slack for their departed coworkers. Unless steps are taken to keep them happy, the organization could be in danger of losing them to exhaustion or low morale, as well. To this end, many organizations are introducing innovative approaches to hold on to experienced people, especially those who possess critical knowledge and talent. For example, some organizations have decided to change their work schedule requirements and permit much more flexibility to accommodate those who have such needs or preferences. According to a recent study by AchieveGlobal, many HR and hiring managers consider the number one area of opportunity to retain talent to be the idea of having a "balanced work–life schedule."[3]

STEP 7: SEEK CONTINUAL SYSTEM FEEDBACK

As with any stage of the Human Capital Cycle, the employee departure stage is not complete without gathering feedback from the employee departure program. Without feedback, adjustments and improvements cannot be made. Worse yet, problems will go unrecognized. So as the final step in the process, the senior management team must plan to keep the lines of communication open in the future.

This stage is an especially critical time to track employee engagement and all other feedback. The organization needs to be made aware of any early cues regarding the pull-back of effort, general employee disenchantment, or early retirement. The earlier the cues are noted, the sooner they can be acted upon.

This concern is especially important when it comes to critical knowledge and talent performers who either have been given competitive offers from other firms or stand to retire soon.

This stage of the Human Capital Cycle presumes positive intent, especially in recognizing the contributions of critical knowledge and talent performers. By delivering on the stated Employee Value Proposition at this stage, the organization is much more likely to engage the employee, whether departing or remaining on board. With such positive intentions, the departing employee becomes a more willing partner in the transfer of deep working knowledge to others in a timely and complete way. This tends to stimulate goodwill with the departing employee and permit other employees to more confidently and competently sustain the contribution of the critical knowledge and talent. Also, if these steps are completed, the organization will avoid experiencing a lapse in benefit to its customers and its bottom line.

EMPLOYEE DEPARTURE STRATEGIES AT WORK

Diane Limon thought she had it all figured out. Her company had undergone monumental changes in recent years and it still seemed to be holding on to its critical talent. Its biggest architects had decided to remain on board despite concerns that they may flee to other companies or to their own agendas. Better yet, more and more people were coming in to the company to add their own contributions. And with the competition faltering, the future looked bright once again.

But there is a problem with always looking forward. If one doesn't take the time to look in the rearview once in a while, one stands to miss everything left in one's wake. With all of Sky International's tremendous success, Limon and the executive board spent nearly a year ignoring the steadily increasing amount of turnover in almost every department. In several offices across the United States, the employees were experiencing discontent, anger, resentment, and frustration. With each crop of new employees coming in every month, the company began to grow more and more alienated from itself. The more the seasoned employees looked around, the more they felt they didn't recognize anyone. And none of these new people seemed to be doing things the old way!

Quality of service began to dissolve. Limon didn't hear it from her employees, either. She heard it from a customer. One of her most loyal and significant customers.

When she presented the predicament to the Human Resource team, she found many of them to be a little jaded on the subject. In the weeks that would follow, she would find the HR team increasingly distracted and prone to gossip, backbiting, mistrust, and ultimate failure. Where once the executive board room had seemed so harmonious, suddenly the environment was nothing short of toxic. Despite all her best efforts, Limon had a disaster on her hands.

The problem was that with all these new faces, HR had trouble maintaining the promises of the Employee Value Proposition. All that goodwill had completely evaporated. Even Human Resources itself, the department that was supposed to serve as the ideal model of a high-performance work group, was now the subject of banter and criticism by other wings of the company. Employees who needed Human Resource services began attempting to find other ways to get their needs met. Worse yet, a number of employees chose to find other employers.

That's when Limon began to get serious about this stage of the Human Capital Cycle. She sat down with the HR team and smoothed out their differences. Then, she took the seven steps to creating a new philosophy of taking good care of the people, whether new or veteran. Once this stage was implemented—and the Human Capital Cycle was complete—the problems began to turn around. Slowly but surely, Sky International returned to its peak as one of the premier architectural firms for which to work. Quantity of new hires began to be replaced by quality. And in the months and years that followed, Sky's turnover rate operated at below 5 percent. This was especially significant because the rest of the industry experienced turnover at four times that rate.

By making an investment to keep her current employees happy and productive, Limon found less need to hire scores of new employees to serve as replacements for the continuously departing people. In the end, her investment paid dividends. With a complete and functional Human Capital Cycle, Limon saved her company tens of millions of dollars.

How does she know how much the turnover agenda saved? She used a tool developed by AchieveGlobal to estimate the cost of employee turnover. The following worksheet includes a calculation that accounts for decreased productivity, the cost of the vacancy, and the cost to hire a replacement employee. It is important to note that this example does not include a calculation for the impact on the business or customers with the loss of a critical knowledge and talent performer. That business impact should be considered to be far higher than this calculation can demonstrate.

SUMMARY

While it might seem like a cast-off stage, given that it deals with employee departure, this final stage of the Human Capital Cycle is just as important as

Table 9.1

Potential Cost of Employee Turnover

Pre-departure			
a.	Average compensation for two weeks	$	
b.	Amount of decreased productivity (0% to 100%)	%	
c.	Cost of lower productivity	(a × b) =	$
d.	Compensation to manager to process separation		$
e.	Compensation to HR to process separation		$
f.	Pre-departure costs	(c + d + e) =	$
Vacancy			
g.	Advertising the vacancy		$
h.	Payments to search firm		$
i.	Interview expenses (dollar value of time to interview)		$
j.	Interview expenses (travel and entertainment)		$
k.	Average number of weeks to fill vacancy	#	
l.	Average weekly overtime to compensate for vacancy or weekly compensation to temp agency	$	
m.	Extra compensation to cover vacant position	(k × l) =	$
n.	Costs incurred during vacancy	(g + h + i + j + m) =	
New Hires			
o.	Average weekly compensation for filled position	$	
p.	Number of weeks in orientation and initial training	#	
q.	Compensation for orientation	(o×p) =	$
r.	Average sign-on bonus		$
s.	Moving allowance		$
t.	Compensation for first month following orientation (o) × (4.33)	$	
u.	Average performance level during first month following orientation (0% to 100%)	%	
v.	Value received with the first month's learning curve	(t × u) =	$
w.	Value lost with the first month's learning curve (v − w)	(t − v) =	$
x.	Costs incurred with new hires	(q + r + s + w) =	$
Total Cost			
Potential cost of employee turnover		(f + n + x) =	$

the others. If carefully administered, the steps listed in this chapter can prevent significant, unanticipated costs.

If the following actions are taken, employee departure will not affect an organization's potential to achieve the Triple Win:

1. Identify or anticipate possible departures of all types
2. Effectively plan for the transfer of working knowledge from current employees to others
3. Determine the mission critical skills and knowledge that must be preserved
4. Efficiently gather useful exit data and use that data in future planning
5. Prepare people to effectively and respectfully assume the roles of departing employees, irrespective of the reasons for the departure
6. Take steps to promote a positive reputation for the organization (including better implementation of the Employee Value Proposition)
7. Establish ongoing goodwill or service relationships with departing employees.

10

OBSERVATIONS, INSIGHTS, AND REFLECTIONS

THANKS IN LARGE PART to her healthy level of foresight, Diane Limon has helped to steer her company away from would-be disaster. Despite slumping levels of leadership in the field and despite the lack of experience on the ground, Sky International has managed to keep its Human Capital needs operating at a near optimum level—even as its competition has begun to falter.

She saw through to the point that her company was in need of a new working strategy for Human Capital Management. And with the aid of her capable CFO, Harold Stevenson, she has managed to help her company achieve this new strategy and generate exactly the kind of results they had hoped for. The plan has been firmly rooted enough in the organization that even Stevenson's pending retirement is unlikely to slow the company down. His leadership will be missed, but since he has taken wholeheartedly to training his own replacement, Sky International can rest assured that the future looks just as bright.

At every level of the company, in fact, the future looks bright. The recruitment and selection program has extended well beyond the new sales force. As that sales force continues to generate new projects in the fresh market space, every role of the company has been infused with more and more capable individuals who operate at a high level as well as appreciate and respect the Employee Value Proposition. The pool of draftsmen and draftswomen has been re-energized. The high-level architects have been diversified. And everything from accounting to Human Resources is operating in a much more efficient and harmonious way.

The program to bring employees on board and orient them has gone as smoothly as the company could have hoped. Continual feedback from multiple streams has kept the process in a state of regular adaptation and continual improvement. As a result, a substantial number of new hires have become capable and highly motivated employees. And this agenda has carried on and will continue to carry on through the life of every employee, regardless of service time. With the power of the EVP and the career growth opportunities set in place by the executive team, Limon can rest easy knowing that her company will remain in capable hands for years to come.

Even in the event of employee departure, Sky International has gotten to the point where its executive team learns and adapts to its mistakes. Holes are filled quickly and gaps in critical talent stand far less significant than they would have been before. Losing a Steven Lions, for example, will not hurt nearly as much as it would have before. But then, Lions does not seem quite as ready to leave the company as he used to be.

When asked what the Human Capital Cycle has meant to her organization, Limon has a hard time overstating its significance. Even during the first year of implementing the plan, she immediately saw the impact of the cycle on the organization, its employees, and its customers. She grasped the Triple Win from the very start. And in the end, her company has saved bundles of money on its hiring, training, and on-boarding efforts while raking it in on a substantial increase in productivity and quality of product. Limon now knows that on the day of her retirement, she can look back at two substantial achievements. The first? Building a Fortune 500 company from the ground up. The second? Keeping it profitable, functional, and highly capable even in a climate of declining Human Capital quality. She stands today almost as proud of implementing the Human Capital Cycle as she is of founding Sky International.

CRITICAL TALENT: THE CORE OF A BUSINESS

The story of Sky International highlights one important overarching lesson: The capability and capacity of an organization to deliver targeted results and sustain long-term economic viability depends upon focused, strategic planning; but more than that, it depends highly upon the organization's ability to manage the bench strength of its leaders and critical knowledge and talent performers.

As such, Human Capital Management must now be considered nothing short of a core business issue. Because the impact of human capital lies at or near the center of nearly every strategic decision, it warrants broader executive involvement beyond the traditional relegation to the Human Resource function. In almost all cases, if a set of key executives takes on an active role in Human Capital Management, the organization effectively seizes more opportunities and thrives. Research results show stronger performance metrics. The organization, its customers, and its employees all experience positive impact. And the Triple Win is realized.

This Human Capital Cycle was created to provide a practical model that is more strategic, comprehensive, and integrated with the needs of the business and its customers. It was intentionally structured to be larger in scope than today's typically more narrow definition of talent management or more constrained view of attracting, developing, and keeping people. This large scope has a way of leading to a more simplified Human Capital Management process over the long term.

The Human Capital Cycle presents the complete approach to activating business strategies and achieving stronger results through people. To support this point, a reflection on the reaction of several organizations that have already been exposed to the Human Capital Cycle is warranted. The organizations represent a variety of industry sectors, both public and private.

SOFTWARE DEVELOPMENT ORGANIZATION[1]

This exploratory case study was completed with a software development start-up organization. The firm was formed in March, 2000, by a venture capitalist and technologist, both of whom planned to develop specific Applications Service Provider (ASP) software. Even as the organization grew to twenty people in the early months, the original business model wasn't realizing enough market traction or revenue for the founders' tastes. In response to this problem, in January, 2001, the team recruited a new chief executive officer with an impressive background in startup and software development situations. With his help and expertise, the new set of key players concluded that the original business model was not going to produce a sustainable market position. Furthermore, they determined that they had to do something quickly, as their funding was rapidly depleting.

By spring of 2001, the organization had conceived an idea for another new software product platform. Market research confirmed an unoccupied market niche, signaling the potential for this new product to be highly lucrative. The research findings also clarified the need for a different marketing and sales approach to the targeted customers.

Armed with these insights, the organization made progress on the new business plan, securing an OEM agreement and another round of venture capital funding by fall of 2001. A number of key players were replaced—including a chief software architect—in order to better address the new product platform. Several more software engineers were hired and turned over in the following months.

While senior management was relatively happy with the progress, they were certainly disappointed with the high turnover rate of employees. Not only was it likely hindering progress and lowering the quality of the software, but also it had begun to cost them a great deal of their investment money. Finding and training replacement employees is a high-cost venture, after all. Many new employees would suggest a deep working knowledge of specific software programs—which would of course lead to their hiring—but would then demonstrate a lack of said knowledge as soon as they began project work.

Many of the senior technical people were making the issue even murkier by continually declaring that the product development was on track. Upon closer examination by senior management, however, it was eventually discovered the whole effort had lagged seriously behind product performance and scheduled targets. This discovery prompted additional employee turnover —as well as a keen desire on the part of the executive team to break the cycle of losing rare and high-performing talent.

Simultaneously, the new CEO voiced ambitions to grow the organization rapidly, but in an orderly way. His theory was that it would help the company capitalize on the highly attractive market position of its products and services. With strong encouragement from its investors, the organization raced to secure a first-to-market position without unnecessarily wasting or squandering its resources.

PROCESS OF THE STUDY

This researcher was invited to explore the situation based upon findings and results from similar, previous research. In initial conversations with the chief executive officer and chief financial officer, the researcher learned that no one in senior management roles had a clear grasp of the explicit Critical Knowledge Areas required to realize the proposed product platform. They stated that this lack of clarity had repeatedly impaired their ability to manage the recruitment and product development process. The executives were uncertain about what questions to ask, what unique measures to monitor, and how to accurately gauge their technical progress. They were also unclear whether their classic stage-gate product development process and detached quality assurance practices were organized to drive best outcomes and efficiently derive the best outputs from application of their Critical Knowledge Areas. They also didn't know how to recruit with sufficient precision to ensure the best staffing for the admittedly unusual product platform.

These initial revelations prompted the creation of a comprehensive approach designed to define critical talent and apply it at an urgent pace. For the data collection end of the creation agenda, analysis included an in-depth inquiry into the business planning documentation as well as interviews with key officers and subject experts. The purpose of this initiative was to define critical talent needs that would drive the performance of the business. The investigation also pursued potential gaps in the existing strategy, processes, systems, policies, and practices.

The study began with a thorough examination of key strategic targets. This activity required a careful and quite different look at the business, given that the purpose was to identify the critical knowledge already at work. To meet this end, the primary focus of the study centered on two points: the core mission of the business and why customers might choose to do business with the organization.

Based on the preliminary findings about the business and its strategic approach, the next step required in-depth discussions with key officers and subject experts. This data gathering process sought insights from people who had expertise on:

- The identity of potential critical knowledge that significantly contributed to the business mission, the value proposition with customers, and other key strategic targets
- The identity of a potential talent profile of the experience, education, professional credentials, and behaviors that are often associated with that knowledge
- Challenges and issues to consider as the organization pursued a more deliberate approach to talent management.

Thorough analyses of this combination of findings produced a set of talent definitions that would directly contribute to the way this organization conducted business in the future.

FINDINGS OF THE STUDY

The findings of the study included a set of Critical Knowledge Areas, definition of critical talent, a set of measures for calculating potential Return on Critical Talent, conclusions about the findings, and specific recommendations for applying these findings to the organization's management techniques, strategies, processes, and systems. The findings were organized in a flow network diagram to trace the source areas and conclusions. Figure 10.1 is a copy of the diagram, excluding the detailed findings.

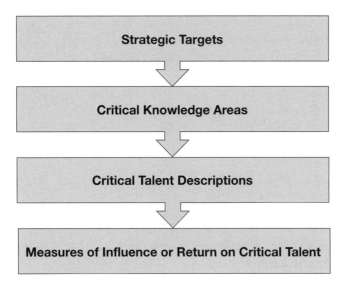

Figure 10.1
Return on Critical Talent: Flow Network Diagram

The Critical Knowledge Areas for this software development startup organization included:

- Comprehensive knowledge of the specific product family software architecture, platform, code interfaces, system integrators, and development methodology
- Research, new product development, and quality assurance processes that fit the customers' acceptance criteria in this product family
- In-depth understanding of the current market and future trends for the "real-time enterprise" and its highly integrated operations, business process software systems, and installed base footprint—plus how to translate those insights into profitable economics for this business type.

The way this organization came to describe its critical talent included a combination of any of the above Critical Knowledge Areas with specific educational, work experience, and behaviors that could best drive the targeted performance results. With this information in mind, the executive team was able to better match an employee's educational depth and type of work experience with the roles requiring a certain level of technical expertise and an accelerated development schedule. For example, certain critical talent required a master's degree level of formal education combined with six to eight years of specific experience, while others could be accommodated by a bachelor's degree level with four or more years of targeted experience.

A behavioral analysis of the business situation and desired culture of this software development startup produced a set of key behaviors that are most likely to effectively stimulate profitable activation of the Critical Knowledge Areas. These behaviors are as follows:

- Drive for results
- Tolerance for ambiguity
- Personal maturity
- Prudent risk taking
- Sense of urgency
- High performance standards
- Self-discipline
- Thorough follow-through with granularity on multiple tasks
- Team leadership of accelerated, complex tasks
- Quality orientation
- Customer service orientation (internal and external).

The research also produced a set of behaviors that this organization's ideal customers would demonstrate in order to extract optimum value from the software products. It was recommended that these behaviors be reflected in the software development organization to create an important, compatible cultural alignment with potential customers. The customer behaviors were posited as follows:

- Keen attention to accurate, real-time data
- Fact-based, streamlined decision making
- Fast learning and knowledge sharing culture
- Fiscal responsibility
- Focus on the requirements that are critical to quality
- Drive for efficiency, effectiveness, and measurable results.

The research findings extracted a number of potential measures of influence or Return on Critical Talent, as well. The list includes:

- Meeting or exceeding the customer's technical and critical-to-quality criteria
- Availability of the software at the targeted time and proficiency level
- Capability to capture and effectively influence the targeted software market space
- Increase the efficiency of internal and external processes and transactions
- Increase in return factors such as revenue, operating margin, and investor equity

- Improvement in human performance scorecard metrics such as revenue per full-time equivalent employee (FTE), turnover, operating margin per FTE, and the direct-to-support ratio.

CONCLUSIONS OF THE STUDY

Upon further analysis of the findings, a number of conclusions related to achieving Return on Critical Talent emerged for this software development startup organization. They were as follows:

- The organization's management deserved recognition for its realization of the need for reconstructing its business model, as well as the quality of its most recent strategic planning, market analysis, and determination to pursue a "first-strike" market position. There was evidence of robust market intelligence and reliance upon the genius of unprecedented, sophisticated software system capabilities.
- The warp-speed race to market was accompanied by the need for fiscal responsibility with venture capital funds. At the same time, they were experiencing expensive, high turnover of rare talent.
- The organization was struggling in its pursuit and formation of a stable, creative, and productive culture, plus refinement of consistent processes, systems, and practices.
- A comprehensive, accelerated approach to culture definition, selection criteria, performance management, setting expectations, coaching, feedback, and reinforcement can yield a focused, energetic workforce of critical talent that clearly understands how individual and group contributions can drive the desired business performance.
- There appeared to be an acute need for a shared, strategic focus among all key leaders, across all functions, and geographies. This condition did not exist at the time of the study to the degree that it must in order to predictably achieve critical milestones and targeted business performance.
- There was uncertainty regarding whether the management group had unanimous conviction about the key strategic targets or how to apply resources to drive specific strategies.

RECOMMENDATIONS

A number of specific recommendations for action were generated from further analysis of the findings. These recommendations were included in a detailed written summary and discussed at length with the chief executive officer of the organization. The recommendations were focused on how to apply the findings to achieve greater Return on Critical Talent while constructively addressing the immediate, urgent business situation that existed. The recommendations included the following:

- Create a clear, crisp, differentiating Customer Value Proposition that directly targets the greatest critical-to-quality customer factors, focuses the product design and development criteria, drives the market strategy, and shapes the emerging market—all while serving to prioritize and leverage its talent resources.
- Examine how product development and quality assurance processes may need to be combined and adjusted to more directly support the unique customer criteria and Critical Knowledge Areas' efficiency and effectiveness.
- Create an Employee Value Proposition that clearly describes and differentiates the firm's employment opportunity and can be effectively used to attract, develop, deploy, and retain critical talent.
- Isolate three to five Critical Success Factors (CSFs) that serve as individual and organizational management focal points to drive for specific performance and verifiable results.
- Practice a high-frequency performance management approach with weekly dialogue at all levels to ensure focus on CSF-related actions.
- Diligently recruit and retain critical talent that will consistently demonstrate the organizational values while urgently delivering concrete business results.
- Apply an assessment process to more precisely discern the fit and degree of technical capabilities (Critical Knowledge Areas) of employment candidates.
- Manage the internal distractions of non-critical activities and issues. Focus organizational energy on product development and customer acquisition to achieve specific, measurable business goals and ensure financial viability.
- Develop a level, internal playing field for all forms of recognition and reward. Recognize and dissolve internal competitive and resource-access tensions that have arisen. Establish baseline compensation and promotion policies and practices to avoid the perception of unfair treatment, unproductive negotiations, hostage behavior, and unbecoming rivalry that undermines teamwork and collaboration among eager, competitive contributors. Create an organizational system where everyone can win.
- Establish a balanced scorecard for measuring progress and managing performance to focus on the investors, market or customers, operational efficiency, and Return on Critical Talent. Load it with metrics that directly

match the Customer and Employee Value Propositions. Cascade the scorecard to every employee to create clear direction and stimulate a stronger sense of personal contribution.

- Conduct and continually monitor a census of critical talent, using the new definitions. Map the Critical Knowledge Areas and critical talent that resides within key strategic processes, functions, and locations.
- Apply the findings to immediate and near-term staffing needs or reassignments to optimally leverage the talent to meet urgent business needs. Immediately target employees who can arrive with the stated critical talent and have a track record of performance in similar circumstances. Given the urgent business situation, there is too much at stake to risk developing critical talent on the job.
- Guide project teams and team leaders to understand and maximize the Return on Critical Talent.
- Use the approach to identify and develop current and future leaders.
- Build Return on Critical Talent into the leadership role and performance management systems.
- Determine the optimal bench strength for critical talent at defined stages of organizational growth and maturity.
- Incorporate Critical Knowledge Areas and critical talent within intellectual property definitions, policies, and practices.
- Create practical tools for monitoring progress, interpreting data, making fact-based decisions to the degree possible—all while tracking managers' performance on goals for managing critical talent.
- Use the critical knowledge and critical talent definitions as specific targets for any retention strategies.
- Establish a process for periodic evaluation of progress on Return on Critical Talent.
- Brief the board of directors or investors on the purpose, importance, and potential impact of Return on Critical Talent, including findings in periodic board reviews.

RESULTS TO DATE

The senior management team of the software startup company pondered the results of the study and took immediate action on several of the points. Within 180 days of the study, a number of positive improvements occurred:

- Selected software engineers created an assessment tool for use in recruitment to discern the technical Critical Knowledge Area capabilities of candidates with greater precision. Recent hires have demonstrated greater capability to create additional product functionality and repair software bugs more rapidly.

- The turnover of critical talent has been significantly reduced from 50 percent to 5 percent.

- Frequent full-staff communications have been instituted. At least weekly discussions with more candid dialogue are held. Teamwork and collaboration are expected and modeled among all levels.

- Key sources of organizational discontent, such as the perception of fair and equitable treatment of employees, civility among key players, and greater role clarity have been constructively addressed. Open discussions of the effect of such issues have led to the creation and application of selected, uniform practices in specific areas.

- Product development has moved from a stall-out condition to producing customer acceptable product performance. Software "bugs" are promptly and cooperatively addressed by product development and quality assurance within its refined, combined process. A greater percentage of product development dates are being met on time.

- The quality of communications and extent of feedback from customers have improved. Technical employees have been working more effectively with sophisticated, discerning, prospective customers. Questions and concerns about the organization's capabilities have been addressed constructively with less tension and a demonstrated willingness to reconfigure within guidelines to meet customer needs.

- There have been numerous, explicit, lengthy discussions among senior technical and marketing management players to constructively address their roles and actions to manage organizational talent, combine customer needs and quality requirements within the product development process, secure more reliable forecasts, conduct daily conversations with direct reports within and across boundaries, and promptly address performance issues.

- The key marketing and distribution channel has secured closure with a number of significant customer opportunities.

- Revenues are expected to exceed earlier forecasts.

- The venture capitalists are encouraging an accelerated round of fundraising to fuel further growth and even stronger market positioning.

IMPLICATIONS FOR OTHER TECHNOLOGY-INTENSIVE ORGANIZATIONS

This case study provides a rich source of findings with important revelations for consideration by other technology-intensive organizations. Such organizations likely rely heavily on specific technical skills and wise interpretation of market and customer intelligence to make important decisions in highly accelerated timeframes.

The study methodology can be easily applied to other situations. The sequence of investigation can produce a comprehensive checklist for diagnosis with other organizations.

While Return on Critical Talent as a model—or series of organizational inquiries and management practices—can produce an important and valuable perspective on any organization, it has unique implications for those that are technology intensive. Very often, technology-intensive organizations tend to concentrate management attention on the technology itself, a few technical targets, and conventional perspectives of personnel credentials. They often struggle with the efficient acquisition and retention of talent. The pressure for results, the urgency to get product to market, and impatient investment sources often tempt the organization in question to engage in costly talent management shortcuts.

But talent management produces desirable results! Organizations that deliver results on their brilliant strategies all have one thing in common: they deliberately engage their people to use the right knowledge, skills, and behaviors at the right time.

The second case study will be drawn from a presentation called "Achieving Return on Critical Talent in Technology-Intensive Organizations." This presentation was given by Dr. Joyce A. Thompsen to the 2002 IEEE International Engineering Management Conference at St. John's College, Cambridge UK on August 18–20, 2002.

HEALTHCARE MANAGEMENT ORGANIZATION

In this case study, the chief executive officer of the healthcare management organization quickly recognized the importance of talent management. The CEO and other members of its leadership team understood that the firm's success was dependent on its ability to create and nurture a culture that continuously scouted for talent and diligently developed and applied that talent for the benefit of its customers and its business. The new realities of its competitive environment required greater management focus and commitment to the performance of associates. Furthermore, the leadership team knew that they had a primary role in ensuring that the organization had both the breadth and depth of talent needed to succeed.

With this in mind, this healthcare management organization undertook a comprehensive approach to pursuing a focus on talent management. The ultimate goal was to create an organizational culture that provided a common understanding of what its talent was, where it might be falling short on said talent, and then finally, how to leverage that talent to meet the specific needs of the organization's customers (who happened to be spread across a multi-state area).

The approach included three phases:

- Phase 1: Defining critical talent needs that drive the performance of the business
- Phase 2: Conducting an organizational census
- Phase 3: Applying those census findings to a full range of talent strategies, processes, systems, and measures.

For a full illustration of this organization's Return on Critical Talent project, see Figure 10.2.

Phase 1 began with a thorough examination of key strategic targets. This activity required a careful and quite different look at the business. The primary focus was upon the core mission of the business and why customers chose to do business with the organization in the first place. Then, all of the key strategic targets were reviewed.

Based on the preliminary findings about the business and its strategic approach, the next step required in-depth discussions with a cross-section sample of people. This data gathering process sought insights from associates who had expertise on:

- The identity of potential critical knowledge that significantly contributed to the business mission, the value proposition with customers, and other key strategic targets
- The identity of a potential talent profile of the experience, education, professional credentials, and behaviors that could very effectively activate that knowledge
- Challenges and issues to consider as the organization pursued a more deliberate approach to talent management.

Thorough analyses of this combination of findings produced a set of talent definitions that were unique to the way the organization conducted business. Since it was engaged in a complex healthcare management business, a number of primary talent definitions were identified. They also determined a number of supporting sources of talent that combined to produce the same results as the primary talent. In this way, the organization expected to uncover even more talent potential.

In Phase 2, the organization created and conducted a talent census (or inventory process). The purpose was to invite all associates to self-declare their current skills and knowledge.

It should be pointed out that the organization took great care in crafting internal communications with its leaders and associates. This proved necessary in order to assure people of the sincere intent to discover, develop, and more strategically apply hidden talent. The leaders also wanted to openly invite all associates to participate in the search for certain types of talent. Today, this openness continues to be important to the organization's culture and clearly signals the desire for fair consideration.

The initial census process identified people who had the defined talent, as well as where they were located within strategic business units, functions, or geographic locations. New opportunities were being identified for employees to apply their experience and knowledge.

Phase 3 continues to this day. The census data has been organized in a database that is used in a variety of ways. The leadership team continues to identify key targets for immediate, near-term, and long-term staffing needs. Both internal and external recruitment strategies are being shaped to meet these needs. In other cases, people are being considered for reassignments as alternatives to meeting important business needs.

The census findings have also proved helpful in identifying potential future leaders and developing important management bench strength. Key candidates include associates who demonstrate strong performance, fit the required talent profile, and possess a keen interest in development opportunities.

The development curriculum continues to be examined, as well. The primary focus of this organization's development agenda is to apply the talent formula noted above: to multiply the effect of knowledge, skills, and behavior by the number and quality of opportunities presented for development and practical experience.

In addition, project team assignments, career rotations, and full or part-time roles are being structured to provide opportunities to serve, teach, or learn. These assignments are now being structured to facilitate shared knowledge and experience.

Members of the leadership team and all other leaders in the organization are being asked to focus on these talent definitions. This includes seeking out opportunities to provide coaching, feedback, and mentoring others. Leaders throughout the regionally dispersed organization are expected to engage in more focused day-to-day performance management in order to ensure the

Strategic Targets and Descriptors	*Mission Statement* *To improve the health of the people we serve*		*Value Proposition (not available)*	
	Strategic Objective Statement Organization will be among the best and biggest in our industry by delivering the best product value with the best people		**Strategic Objectives** • Achieve the targeted performance characteristics of our best competitors in each region • Increase our scale and market share in targeted regions • Create competitive edge through product value • Become the employer of choice in the health management industry and in targeted regions	**Operating Imperatives** • Grow profitable enrollment • Reduce administrative cost • Reduce cost of care • Improve the health of our members • Improve the level of service • Develop our associates
	Organization's Core Values • Customer Focus • Commitment to Excellence • Continuous Improvement and Innovation • Results with Integrity • Teamwork		**Four "Fs"** 1. Fast 2. Fun 3. Flexible 4. Focused	**Six "Cs"** 1. Capability 2. Commitment 3. Contribution 4. Continuity 5. Collaboration 6. Conscience
Potential Critical Knowledge Areas	Knowledge of the economics of our healthcare insurance business and systemic influences among members (employers), provider network, clinical/medical care	Knowledge of actuarial and underwriting practices in determining rates that meet the needs of both our customers and organization (31)	Collective knowledge about our targeted markets, competition, and our customer relationships (24)	Knowledge about how to translate customer needs into profitable business (risk assessment and management) for organization (12)	CKA Needed: Knowledge about how to effectively do our business through e-commerce

	management, interested public parties, and organization (34)			
Potential Critical Talent Descriptions	**Experience** • Healthcare industry insurance experience • Healthcare system experience of any type (brokerage, medical care management, insurance, etc.) • Work experience within multiple functions in healthcare (or within organization)	**Education and/or Professional Credentials** • Actuarial credentials • Medical/clinical credentials • Appropriate licensure with state departments of insurance	**Behavioral Profile** • Strategic, systemic thinking with short/long term view • Critical thinking and creative problem solving • Disciplined analysis, judgment, and decisiveness • Willingness to take initiative • Personal and professional credibility • Ability to communicate complex situations with clarity • Collaboration	**Behavioral Profile** • Accountability and drive for results • Willingness to share information • Ability to identify meaningful patterns and opportunities • Flexibility and openness to change • High standards of excellence • Sense of urgency • Change leader • Customer service orientation (internal and external) • Ability to influence others to action
Potential Measures of Influence or Return on Critical Talent	Efficiency and effectiveness of the combination of Critical Knowledge Areas and critical talent may produce the following potential changes: • Reduction in internal and external transaction cost factors • Increase in effect of deep knowledge about the triangle and systemic effects • Increase in return factors such as revenue, operating margins, and sales • Increase in customer loyalty and market share			

Figure 10.2
Healthcare Management Organization—Return on Critical Talent Project: Flow Network Diagram

effective deployment of talent. The criteria for promotions, rewards, and performance recognition are also being realigned.

In the midst of this focused management attention to processes, systems, and daily practices, the leadership team recognizes the strong correlation with its cultural strategy. By words and actions, all leaders are expected to heighten the awareness and sense of urgency for the proactive stewardship of talent.

IN CONCLUSION

Unfortunately, for years, not nearly enough organizations followed the examples of the above two case studies. Far too few have taken the hands-on approach demonstrated by Diane Limon and Sky International. Few organizations currently deploy any form of succession planning, talent management, building leadership bench strength, watching critical knowledge and talent performers, or engaging in an overarching Human Capital Management strategy.

But this is not for lack of need. Most often, it is for lack of focus on the part of the executive team. Chalk this up to the general underestimation of the importance of Human Capital Management as a core business strategy. For many companies, the executive teams have not yet started monitoring the potential peril of insufficient or ineffective Human Capital Management. Their executives don't know about the compelling case. They don't know the potential impact on their own organization. They have no idea who their critical knowledge and talent performers are—or where they are—or the even the value that they bring. They haven't given much, if any, thought to the potential impact on keeping the value proposition with their constituents or customers.

The potential Triple Win does not exist in their lexicon.

The good news: people are now becoming equipped with facts and evidence that will drive wiser executive decisions and activate much greater personal involvement in Human Capital Management. Adoption of the Human Capital Cycle is one of the smart choices.

11

QUESTIONS TO CONSIDER

Many times, members of the senior management team are new to the arena of Human Capital Management. In our experience, we have found that the questions included in this appendix serve as excellent primers to get the process of gathering information started. These questions will prove abundantly valuable for any organization hoping to implement the Human Capital Cycle in order to realize the benefits of the Triple Win.

CHAPTER 1

Globalization and the need for an international workforce:

- What are the principal strategic drivers that require the organization to undertake globalization and the installation of an international workforce?
- What are the intended benefits to the customers, the organization, and both current and proposed employees?
- What combination of skills, knowledge, motivations, experience, education, language capabilities, cultural expression, and locale are required to fulfill the globalization strategy?
- What affect will the choice, preparation, and capabilities of the international workforce have on delivering the Customer Value Proposition?
- What central operating model and infrastructure will be installed, and to what degree will those be compatible and effective with the existing organization?
- How will the organization select and orient an international workforce to meet the full expectations for performance, or perhaps accelerate results?
- What opportunities will be provided for current employees to grow and develop with assignments in the international scene?

Organizational growth:

- What is the core definition of organizational growth? Is the definition confined to developing a profitable revenue stream with choices for fulfillment by organic means or acquisition?
- How far and how fast does the organization need to grow in order to achieve the targeted results?
- How will we monitor our growth to ensure we are on a sound trajectory?
- What are the organizational risks, and how will we mitigate them to safeguard the core business, our position with customers, and current employee population?
- To what degree are accelerated results required by any portion of the organization, in order to accomplish or justify the growth strategy?
- To what degree is geographic expansion and presence in new locations required?
- Does the strategy require the development of new channels and the skills to serve in the market space?
- What new critical knowledge and talent is required to fulfill the strategy?
- Does the organization have sufficient leadership and critical performer bench strength in its talent inventory to undertake all of the roles required by the growth strategy?
- How will the organization become prepared to responsibly undertake the dual stewardship of the current functionalities while growing or expanding?
- What organizational infrastructure is the best fit for the transition to the targeted future size?
- How will Human Capital Management processes, systems, policies, and practices need to adapt to the growth strategy?
- Will internal and external talent markets be activated to fill new positions?
- How will the Customer Value Proposition be affected by the organizational growth strategy? How will all current and new employees be oriented to any adjustments in the Customer Value Proposition?

Similarly, the evolving or transforming cultures scenario is fulfilled by essential attention within Human Capital Management. Sample questions in this category include the following:

- What factors are prompting the realization of a business need to evolve or transform the current organizational culture?
- To what degree does this decision align with valid analytics derived from customers or the market space?
- What precise changes in the culture need to occur?

- How will the pinpointed culture changes become evident in observable or measurable ways within the organization and to customers?
- How will the culture change affect the measurable performance of the organization?
- How will the changes be communicated within the organization, to the market and customers, and other key constituents?
- How do these changes affect the organization's mission, vision, values, and Customer Value Proposition?
- How will the culture change affect the Employee Value Proposition?
- What new skills, knowledge, motivations, abilities, experience, education, and cultural predilections are required?
- How will current employees undertake the targeted cultural shift?
- What is their current change capability for such a shift?
- What actions will all leaders in the organization undertake to enable, promote, coach, reinforce, and monitor the shift?
- How will recruitment and selection strategies need to change?
- How will the cultural shift trigger turnover vulnerability, especially with critical talent performers or high-potential employees?
- What strategy will be used with those employees who express unwillingness to engage in the targeted cultural shift?
- How will we monitor the evolution or transformative culture shift?

Changes in market demands:

- What evidence is signaling a shift in market demand, and what is the nature of the strategic response?
- To what degree will the human capital capabilities of the organization need to shift to seize upon either the opportunities or risks inherent in the changes in market demands?
- What is the nature and availability of critical knowledge and talent required to respond, such as creating innovative or disruptive products and services, changes in approach to the market space, working effectively in new channels, or accelerating product introductions or expirations?
- Does the organization have the talent in inventory to execute the strategy?
- To what degree does the change in market demand require the identification and execution of a new operating model and a translation into new skills, knowledge, abilities, and motivations to apply the model?
- How will the changes in market demands affect the customer decision analytics and trigger new loyalty migration points, which ultimately are fulfilled by a new set of employee behaviors in customer transactions?

- How will sales and service performance models need to adjust? How will the employees be prepared to deliver superior performance?
- How will the organizational infrastructure, roles, and responsibilities need to change to fulfill the strategy?

The trend of retirements has been on the distant horizon for a number of years. As noted in Chapter 1, significant percentages of employees are eligible or enacting retirements in the present tense. This trend is a significant trigger for strategic and tactical Human Capital Management:

- What are the analytics for potential or planned retirements within our own organization?
- What specific mission critical knowledge and talent performers fall within the window of either potential or planned retirements in the near term?
- What are the specific risks to our organization, our customers, and employee groups if we don't have sufficient replacement strength in place on time?
- What actions are required to create broader or transferred coverage of those mission critical knowledge and talent performer roles?
- How can retirements be managed in a sensitive, respectful way that promotes goodwill within the departing employees, with the customers they serve, and other employees?
- How can the organization create opportunities for retirees to comfortably return for any form of bridge or boomerang service?

CHAPTER 2

- How will we create a compelling case for the purpose, importance, and expected impact of a human capital or succession planning and management process that fits the explicit current and future needs of our own organization?
- How will we ground the case with data from thorough business and organizational assessment?
- How will we secure a high level of conviction and active involvement in the process by all senior leaders, led by the CEO?
- How will we crystallize roles and responsibilities for all players?
- How will we confirm the intent to use this process for all open positions?
- How will we set an overarching strategy for building leadership and critical talent performer bench strength: right people with the right skills, in the right place, and at the right time?

- How will we define a meticulous, comprehensive, strategically aligned, fair, and equitable human capital or succession planning and management process that provides opportunities to everyone?
- How will we create a detailed communications plan to accurately portray the full intent of what to expect—and what not to expect?
- How will we identify an accurate list of leadership and critical talent performer competencies (skills, knowledge, abilities, and motivations)—a talent portfolio—that will produce superior performance in the likely future scenarios of the organization?
- How will we identify key mission critical or linchpin positions that can propel or inhibit our strategic initiatives or opportunities?
- How will we use the competencies to assess the current talent pool?
- How will we analyze the results to identify high-potential candidates and critical talent performers and create pinpointed developmental plans?
- How will we align the human capital or succession planning and management process with an Employee Value Proposition—why a promising leader will want to grow, develop, and contribute with this organization over the long term?
- How will we incorporate appropriate messaging in our recruitment strategies?
- How will we create a set of training and developmental experiences that are directly connected to building skill in the leadership and critical talent performer competencies?
- How will we tie the process to the organization's performance management, promotion, reward and recognition, and related Human Resources systems, processes, and policies?
- How will we engage in at least annual reviews with the process and all candidates?
- When there are triggering strategic circumstances, will we conduct an immediate review of the human capital or succession planning and management process to test all assumptions and directions?
- How will we routinely look first to the succession planning, leadership bench strength, or talent inventory for promotional opportunities?
- How will we periodically measure and evaluate the integrity and progress of the process, regulatory compliance, and the movement of high-potential candidates and critical talent performers, turnover and retention strategies, impact of developmental activities, and other metrics that tie to strategic fulfillment?
- How will we communicate and celebrate results?
- How will we include the board of directors, shareholders, or other key stakeholders in critical communications and Human Capital Management direction?

CHAPTER 3

- What's happening within our organization, with the competition, or the marketplace that warrants prompt attention to our talent?
- Do we truly know what Critical Knowledge and Talent drives the highest value with our customers?
- What deliberate processes do we have in place to track the return on that knowledge and talent?
- How many of our organization's leaders thoroughly immerse themselves in the primary task of finding and fully engaging the best talent?
- How do we need to identify and mobilize our talent in order to predictably stay ahead of the competition?
- How do we know which of our associates we can't afford to lose?
- How well are our human resource processes, systems, and practices aligned to identify, develop, and retain talent?
- How do we create a development curriculum that focuses on the key elements of talent and providing the best opportunities for development and gaining experience?
- How well do our product development processes apply our Critical Knowledge Areas and Critical Talent?
- As we reconstruct our organizations, how do we identify associates who can use their knowledge, skills, and behavior to deliver critical value to our customers?
- How do we need to prepare our organizations as valued, knowledgeable, talented contributors move into retirement?
- How do we measure the results of our organization's human performance? What about the contribution of critical talent to our customers?
- What are the risks of taking no action on talent?

CHAPTER 4

- How will we effectively sort competing priorities, points of view, sense of urgency, and limited resources to secure prompt clarity and direction in complex situations?
- How will we build shared ownership of an important, realizable strategy?
- What strategic options do we need to explore? What criteria will we use?
- What risks might we encounter, and how will we mitigate them?
- How will we test the strategy to avoid unintended, unfavorable consequences?
- How will we determine what human capital resources are truly necessary?

- Where do we have strategic vulnerability with critical knowledge and talent?
- How will we communicate effectively to build broad commitment to the strategy, changes required, and responsibility for results?
- How well do our current processes, systems, policies, practices, and culture align with the proposed strategy?
- How will we measure success?
- How will we recognize people and celebrate success?
- How will we set and monitor feedback loops?

CHAPTER 5

- How will we accurately define the skills, knowledge, abilities, and motivations required for superior performance in fulfilling this strategy?
- How will we organize and conduct a census that captures employee capabilities?
- How do the targeted competencies compare with our current capabilities?
- How will we pinpoint gaps for developing internally—or for hiring from outside our organization?
- How will our job profiles need to change?
- How will we be sure our processes, systems, policies, and practices fit the Human Capital plan?
- How will we ensure fair and equitable consideration for current and outside candidates?
- How will we set performance expectations for all leaders to find, fully engage, develop, and retain the right people who fit the Human Capital plan?
- How will we identify mission critical roles and individuals that require special retention strategies?
- How will we test rewards, recognition, and compensation practices to attract the right talent?
- How will we continually secure double-loop feedback and deploy new findings?
- How will we set an evaluation plan to gauge impact?

CHAPTER 6

- How will we ensure we are as effective, efficient, and fair as possible in our recruitment and selection process?
- How will we be confident we are selecting the right people—with skills, knowledge, abilities, and motivations that best fit our needs?

- How will we communicate our Employee Value Proposition in as appealing and compelling way as possible?
- How will we more effectively position our organization's opportunities as compared to others in the external talent market?
- How will we activate an efficient, inclusive, pull-through process in an internal talent market?
- How will we continually gather and deploy feedback?
- How will we ensure we meet human capital deadlines without compromise?

CHAPTER 7

- How will we accelerate commitment, learning, and contributions of new employees to the strategy of the organization?
- How will we design and deliver a clear sequence of learning that produces understanding, comfort, and confidence in a new organization or role—without confusion or inundation with too much detail?
- How will we communicate clear line of sight connections to the strategy and measures of success?
- How will we develop a working knowledge of the organization's mission, vision, and values?
- How will we effectively communicate essential organizational and customer knowledge?
- How will we set up mentors or a social networking system for supporting new employees?
- How will we establish systemic attention to an integrating culture?
- How will we ensure every step fits the Employee Value Proposition?
- How will we verify the degree of employee engagement and support in this early period of employment?
- How will we position the on-boarding within the broader development process throughout the lifecycle?
- How will we secure feedback on the orientation process—and quickly learn what additional help is needed?

CHAPTER 8

- How will we build a comprehensive employee development plan—in timely phases—that meets the needs of the organizational and individual career growth plans?

- How will we engage in formal and informal performance management discussions, coaching, feedback, reinforcement, and recognition to produce superior performance?
- How will we periodically assess and gauge growth?
- How will we continually verify employee engagement, satisfaction, and commitment?
- How will we build in a retention strategy that's meaningful to the employees and saves organizational resources?
- How will we stay apprised of unique generational or professional shifts and requirements?
- How will we continually deliver the Employee Value Proposition experience?
- How will we establish a pull-through strategy in a talent market?
- How will we track system dynamics over time to ensure this stage stays on track?
- How will we ensure our critical talent stays and contributes?
- How will we avoid redundancies, overlap, and outdating in resources?

CHAPTER 9

- How will we identify or anticipate possible departures of all types?
- How will we effectively plan for the transfer of working knowledge from current employees to others?
- What are our mission critical skills and knowledge that we need to preserve? How will we easily and effectively create broader coverage?
- How will we effectively and efficiently gather useful exit data and use that data in future planning?
- How will we prepare people to effectively and respectfully assume the roles of departing employees, irrespective of the reasons?
- How will we evaluate how well we are fulfilling our Employee Value Proposition?
- How will we reduce voluntary turnover to an acceptable level?
- What will we do to promote a positive reputation for the organization?
- What kinds of ongoing good will or service relationships can we establish with departing employees?
- How will we tap into system feedback to gain early alerts to potential unwanted departures?

NOTES

1 INTRODUCTION

1 Business Performance Management Forum. *The 2007 Performance and Talent Management Trend Survey*. Palo Alto, CA: Business Performance Management Forum and SuccessFactors in cooperation with the Human Capital Institute, March, 2007.

2 BROADENING THE HUMAN CAPITAL SPECTRUM

1 Thompsen, Joyce, and Smith, Anne E.P. *Building Leadership Bench Strength: Current Trends in Succession Planning and Management*. AchieveGlobal Research Paper, October, 2005.
2 Michaels, E., Handfield-Jones, H., and Axelrod, B. *The War for Talent*. Boston, MA: Harvard Business School Press, 2001.
3 "The Battle for Brainpower." *The Economist*, October 5, 2006.
4 Statistics gathered from Business Performance Management Forum. *The 2007 Performance and Talent Management Trend Survey*. Palo Alto, CA: Business Performance Management Forum and SuccessFactors in cooperation with the Human Capital Institute, March, 2007.
5 "Retiring Workforce, Widening Skills Gap, Exodus of 'Critical Talent' Threaten U.S. Companies: Deloitte Consulting Survey." *CFO Magazine*, February 15, 2005.
6 Bersin, Josh. *High-Impact Talent Management: State of the Market and Executive Overview*. Bersin & Associates, May, 2007.
7 Poll conducted by AchieveGlobal in June, 2005.
8 Business Performance Management Forum, March, 2007.
9 "CEO Challenges 2004." Conference Board Report, August, 2004.
10 Watson Wyatt. *Human Capital Index Report 2002*. Watson Wyatt Worldwide Research Report, October, 2002.

4 EMERGENCE OF NEW NEED/STRATEGY

1 The Economist Intelligence Unit, *CEO Briefing: Corporate Priorities for 2006 and Beyond*. London: The Economist Intelligence Unit and UK Trade and Investment, 2006. Available at http://a330.g.akamai.net/7/330/2540/20060213185601/graphics.eiu.com/files/ad_pdfs/ceo_Briefing_UKTI_wp.pdf (accessed February 13, 2009).
2 "HR Executive Review Improving the New Employment Compact." Conference Board Report, 1997.
3 Kiger, Patrick J. "Explaining Executives' Dim View of HR." *Workforce Management*, June 26, 2007.

4 Gurthridge, Matthew, Komm, Asmus, and Lawson, Emily. "The People Problem in Talent Management." *The McKinsey Quarterly*, June, 2006.
5 Leibs, Scott. "Measuring Up: Many Companies Still Struggle to Use Metrics Effectively." *CFO Magazine*, June, 2007.
6 Leibs, Scott. "Measuring Up."
7 Leibs, Scott. "Measuring Up."
8 Davenport, Tom and Harris, Jeanne. *Competing on Analytics: The New Science of Winning*. Boston, MA: Harvard Business School, 2007.
9 Ernst & Young. *Measures that Matter*. London: Ernst & Young LLP, 2000.

5 DEFINITION OF THE HUMAN CAPITAL PLAN

1 According to a study conducted by Bersin & Associates, 21 percent of organizations polled reported that they had some form of talent management in place. Of those organizations, only 5 percent reported any level of senior management involvement in the process. Bersin & Associates. *Introducing High-Impact Talent Management Research Findings*. WhatWorks in *Talent Management Newsletter*, May, 2007.
2 Thompsen, Joyce. "Gaining Greater Benefit from Lean Six Sigma and Leadership Initiatives within the Military." *Proceedings of the IEEE International Engineering Management Conference*. St John's, Newfoundland, Canada, September 11, 2005.
3 Thompsen, Joyce, and Smith, Anne E.P. *Building Leadership Bench Strength: Current Trends in Succession Planning and Management*. AchieveGlobal Research Paper, October, 2005. These competencies were identified in research focusing on succession planning and building leadership bench strength and were revealed via survey as common among the pool of respondents when it comes to identifying high-potential employees.

6 RECRUITMENT AND SELECTION

1 Business Performance Management Forum. *The 2007 Performance and Talent Management Trend Survey*. Palo Alto, CA: Business Performance Management Forum and SuccessFactors in cooperation with the Human Capital Institute, March, 2007.
2 "The Battle for Brainpower." *The Economist*, October 5, 2006.
3 Davidson, Glenn, Lepeak, Stan, and Newman, Elizabeth. *The Impact of the Aging Workforce on Public Sector Organizations and Mission*. Alexandria, VA: International Public Management Association for Human Resources (IPMA-HR), February, 2007.
4 Kirsch, Christina. "Loyalty and Disengagement—Taming the Retention Monster." *Australian Management Magazine*, October 1, 2007.
5 Bell, Andrew. "The Employee Value Proposition Redefined." *Strategic HR Review*, 4(4): 3, 2005.
6 This story was based on AchieveGlobal. *New Strategy. New Sales Team. New Problems?* AchieveGlobal Case Study, July, 2003.

7 EMPLOYEE ON-BOARDING AND ORIENTATION

1 Caudron, Shari. "How HR Drives Profits." *Workforce*, 80(12): 26–29, 2001.
2 AchieveGlobal. *Talent Management and Employee Retention Report*. AchieveGlobal Internal Study, March, 2008.
3 "The 'Masculine' and 'Feminine' Sides of Leadership and Culture: Perceptions as Reality." *Knowledge@Wharton*, October 5, 2005.
4 Watkins, Michael. *The First 90 Days*. Boston, MA: Harvard Business School Publishing, 2003.

5 Deloitte. *It's 2008: Do You Know Where Your Talent Is? Connecting People to What Matters.* Deloitte Research Paper 2007.

8 DEVELOPMENT OF ONGOING CAPABILITIES OR CAREER GROWTH

1 Poll conducted by AchieveGlobal in June, 2005.
2 Zaccaro, Stephen J. *The Nature of Executive Leadership: A Conceptual and Empirical Analysis of Success.* Washington, D.C.: American Psychological Association, 2001.
3 Morrow, C. C., Jarrett, M.Q., and Rupinski, M.T. "An Investigation of the Effect and Economic Utility of Corporate-Wide Training." *Personnel Psychology*, 50: 91–119, 1997, cited by Spencer, Lyle M., Jr., "Competency Assessment Methods." In Laurie J., Bassi and Darlene Russ-Eft (eds) *What Works: Assessment, Development, and Measurement.* Alexandria, VA: American Society for Training and Development, 1997.
4 Caudron, Shari. "How HR Drives Profits." *Workforce*, 80(12): 26–29, 2001.
5 "Training Boosts Leadership Skills and Performance in U.S. Health and Human Services Agencies." *Impact!* (AchieveGlobal newsletter) 3(2), 2000.
6 Thompsen, Joyce. *Leading from a Distance: Skills for Success.* AchieveGlobal Research Paper, October, 2000.
7 Ready, Douglas and Conger, Jay. "Make Your Company a Talent Factory." *Harvard Business Review*, June, 2007.
8 Pascale, Richard and Parsons, George. "Crisis at the Summit." *Harvard Business Review*, March, 2007.
9 Bryan, Lowell L. and Joyce, Claudia I. *Mobilizing Minds: Creating Wealth from Talent in the 21st-Century Organization.* New York: McGraw-Hill, 2007; Bryan, Lowell L., Joyce, Claudia I. and Weiss, Leigh M. "Making a Market in Talent." *The McKinsey Quarterly*, June, 2006.
10 Goffee, Rob and Jones, Gareth. "Leading Clever People." *Harvard Business Review*, March, 2007.
11 Corporate Leadership Council. *Hallmarks of Leadership Success: Strategies for Improving Leadership Quality and Executive Readiness.* Washington, D.C.: Advisory Board Company, 2003.

9 EMPLOYEE DEPARTURE

1 AchieveGlobal. *Talent Management and Employee Retention Report.* AchieveGlobal Internal Study, March, 2008.
2 AchieveGlobal. *Talent Management and Employee Retention Report.*
3 AchieveGlobal. *Talent Management and Employee Retention Report.*

10 OBSERVATIONS, INSIGHTS, AND REFLECTIONS

1 The following stories are taken from "A Case Study on Achieving Return on Critical Talent in Technology-Intensive Organizations," a presentation delivered by Dr. Joyce A. Thompsen to the Portland International Conference on Management of Engineering and Technology in Portland, Oregon on July 20–24, 2003.

FURTHER READING

Boudreau, John W. and Ramstad, Peter M. *Beyond HR: The New Science of Human Capital.* Boston, MA: Harvard Business School Publishing, 2007.

Charan, R., Drotter, S., and Noel, J. *The Leadership Pipeline: How to Build the Leadership-Powered Company.* San Francisco, CA: Jossey-Bass, 2001.

Fitz-enz, J. *The ROI of Human Capital: Measuring the Economic Value of Employee Performance.* New York: AMACOM, 2000.

Mankins, M. and Steele, R. "Turning Great Strategy into Great Performance." *Harvard Business Review,* July–August, 2005.

Sterman, John D. *Business Dynamics: Systems Thinking and Modeling for a Complex World.* Boston, MA: Irwin McGraw-Hill, 2000.

Storey, John, Wright, Patrick, and Ulrich, Dave (eds) *The Routledge Companion of Strategic Human Resource Management.* London: Routledge, 2009.

Sullivan, John. "The True Value of Hiring and Retaining Top Performers." Report of the California Strategic HR Partnership. *Workforce: HR Trends and Tools for Business Results.* October 1, 2002.

REFERENCES

AchieveGlobal. *New Strategy. New Sales Team. New Problems?* AchieveGlobal Case Study, July, 2003.

AchieveGlobal. *Talent Management and Employee Retention Report.* AchieveGlobal Internal Study, March, 2008.

Bell, Andrew. "The Employee Value Proposition Redefined." *Strategic HR Review,* 4(4): 3, 2005.

Bersin, Josh. *High-Impact Talent Management: State of the Market and Executive Overview.* Bersin & Associates, May, 2007.

Bersin & Associates. *Introducing High-Impact Talent Management Research Findings.* WhatWorks in *Talent Management Newsletter,* May, 2007.

Bryan, Lowell L. and Joyce, Claudia I. *Mobilizing Minds: Creating Wealth from Talent in the 21st-Century Organization.* New York: McGraw-Hill, 2007.

Bryan, Lowell L., Joyce, Claudia I. and Weiss, Leigh M. "Making a Market in Talent." *The McKinsey Quarterly,* June, 2006.

Business Performance Management Forum. *The 2007 Performance and Talent Management Trend Survey.* Palo Alto, CA: Business Performance Management Forum and SuccessFactors in cooperation with the Human Capital Institute, March, 2007.

Caudron, Shari. "How HR Drives Profits." *Workforce,* 80(12): 26–29, 2001.

"CEO Challenges 2004." The Conference Board Report, August, 2004.

Corporate Leadership Council. *Hallmarks of Leadership Success: Strategies for Improving Leadership Quality and Executive Readiness.* Washington, D.C.: Advisory Board Company, 2003.

Davenport, Tom and Harris, Jeanne. *Competing on Analytics: The New Science of Winning.* Boston, MA: Harvard Business School, 2007.

Davidson, Glenn, Lepeak, Stan, and Newman, Elizabeth. *The Impact of the Aging Workforce on Public Sector Organizations and Mission.* Alexandria, VA: International Public Management Association for Human Resources (IPMA-HR), February, 2007.

Deloitte. *It's 2008: Do You Know Where Your Talent Is? Connecting People to What Matters.* Deloitte Research Paper 2007.

Ernst & Young. *Measures that Matter.* London: Ernst & Young LLP, 2000.

Goffee, Rob and Jones, Gareth. "Leading Clever People." *Harvard Business Review,* March, 2007.

Gurthridge, Matthew, Komm, Asmus, and Lawson, Emily. "The People Problem in Talent Management." *The McKinsey Quarterly,* June, 2006.

"HR Executive Review Improving the New Employment Compact." Conference Board Report, 1997.

Kiger, Patrick J. "Explaining Executives' Dim View of HR." *Workforce Management,* June 26, 2007.

Kirsch, Christina. "Loyalty and Disengagement—Taming the Retention Monster." *Australian Management Magazine,* October 1, 2007.

Leibs, Scott. "Measuring Up: Many Companies Still Struggle to Use Metrics Effectively." *CFO Magazine,* June, 2007.

Michaels, E., Handfield-Jones, H., and Axelrod, B. *The War for Talent.* Boston, MA: Harvard Business School Press, 2001.

Morrow, C. C., Jarrett, M.Q., and Rupinski, M.T. "An Investigation of the Effect and Economic Utility of Corporate-Wide Training." *Personnel Psychology,* 50: 91–119, 1997.

Pascale, Richard and Parsons, George. "Crisis at the Summit." *Harvard Business Review,* March, 2007.

Ready, Douglas and Conger, Jay. "Make Your Company a Talent Factory." *Harvard Business Review,* June, 2007.

"Retiring Workforce, Widening Skills Gap, Exodus of 'Critical Talent' Threaten U.S. Companies: Deloitte Consulting Survey." *CFO Magazine,* February 15, 2005.

Spencer, Lyle M., Jr., "Competency Assessment Methods." In Laurie J. Bassi and Darlene Russ-Eft (eds) *What Works: Assessment, Development, and Measurement.* Alexandria, VA: American Society for Training and Development, 1997.

"The Battle for Brainpower." *The Economist,* October 5, 2006.

The Economist Intelligence Unit, *CEO Briefing: Corporate Priorities for 2006 and Beyond.* London: The Economist Intelligence Unit and UK Trade and Investment, 2006. Available at http://a330.g.akamai.net/7/330/2540/20060213185601/graphics.eiu.com/files/ad_pdfs/ceo_Briefing_UKTI_wp.pdf (accessed February 13, 2009).

"The 'Masculine' and 'Feminine' Sides of Leadership and Culture: Perceptions as Reality." *Knowledge@Wharton,* October 5, 2005.

Thompsen, Joyce. *Leading from a Distance: Skills for Success.* AchieveGlobal Research Paper, October, 2000.

Thompsen, Joyce. "A Case Study on Achieving Return on Critical Talent in Technology-Intensive Organizations." *Portland International Conference on Management of Engineering and Technology Proceedings,* July 20, 2003.

Thompsen, Joyce. "Gaining Greater Benefit from Lean Six Sigma and Leadership Initiatives within the Military." *Proceedings of the IEEE International Engineering Management Conference.* St John's, Newfoundland, Canada, September 11, 2005.

Thompsen, Joyce, and Smith, Anne E.P. *Building Leadership Bench Strength: Current Trends in Succession Planning and Management.* AchieveGlobal Research Paper, October, 2005.

"Training Boosts Leadership Skills and Performance in U.S. Health and Human Services Agencies." *Impact!* (AchieveGlobal newsletter) 3(2), 2000.

Watkins, Michael. *The First 90 Days.* Boston, MA: Harvard Business School Publishing, 2003.

Watson Wyatt. *Human Capital Index Report 2002.* Watson Wyatt Worldwide Research Report, October, 2002.

Zaccaro, Stephen J. *The Nature of Executive Leadership: A Conceptual and Empirical Analysis of Success.* Washington, D.C.: American Psychological Association, 2001.

INDEX

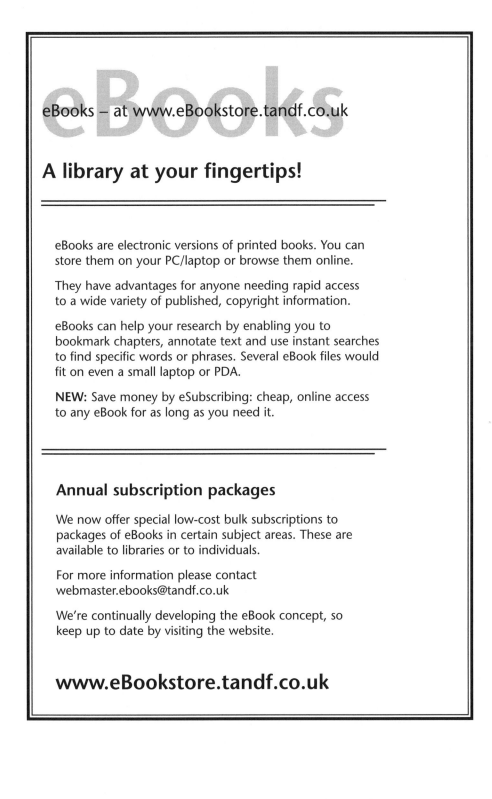